P9-DFL-399

Country

Country

Classic and Contemporary Ideas for Living

BARBARA RADCLIFFE ROGERS

PRICE STERN SLOAN
Los Angeles

A TERN ENTERPRISES BOOK

Published by Price Stern Sloan, Inc.
360 North La Cienega Boulevard, Los Angeles, California 90048

Printed in Hong Kong.
9 8 7 6 5 4 3 2 1

LIBRARY OF CONGRESS CATALOGING-IN-PUBLICATION DATA

Rogers, Barbara Radcliffe.
Country by Barbara Radcliffe Rogers.
p. cm.
Includes index.
ISBN 0-89586-744-3: $24.95
1. Handicraft—United States. 2. Cookery, American.
3. Gardening—United States. 4. Interior decoration—United States—Amateurs' manuals. I. Title.
TT157.R615 1989
745'.0973—dc19 88-36975
CIP

COUNTRY
Classic and Contemporary Ideas for Living
was prepared and produced by
Tern Enterprises, Inc.
15 West 26th Street
New York, New York 10010

Editor: Stephen Williams
Designer: Judy Morgan
Art Director: Robert W. Kosturko
Photography Editor: Christopher Bain
Photo Researcher: Daniella Jo Nilva
Production Manager: Karen L. Greenberg

Typeset by Mar+x Myles Graphics, Inc.
Color separations by Universal Color Scanning Ltd.
Printed and bound in Hong Kong

Dedication

To Norm, whose clambakes were New England's finest and Claire, who can spot a good Johnny-cake pan from fifty paces and whose blackberry pies could inspire poets, with love and fondest memories...

Contents

PLEASANT STREET
INN

© Nancy Hill

© Louis Sahuc/Stock Options

© William Seitz

© Bart Barlow/Envision

© Lynn Karlin

Introduction

Life in the country has moments that cannot be duplicated anywhere else—horses in a fog-covered field at sunrise, the sweet steam of sap boiling into maple syrup on a wood stove, the plaintive call of a whippoorwill lulling you to sleep.

But country living is just as much a way of looking at life as it is actually living in the country. The sweet smell of balsam, the warmth of an heirloom quilt, the taste of fresh bread—all of these country pleasures are as easily savored in an apartment high above the bustling city as they are in a log cabin deep in the woods.

This book is for those who treasure the richness of country living, whether their country hideaway is on San Francisco's Telegraph Hill, or in Blue Hills, Maine; in an apartment tower in Vancouver, or on a farm near Thunder Bay.

The history of the country style is the history of North America itself, drawn from the thatched cottages and country houses of England, the German immigrants we call Pennsylvania Dutch, the Spanish influence typified in Santa Fe, the French Canadians in Quebec and the rich culture of the Native North Americans. The particular style of North American country is firmly rooted in the very spirit of the land.

In the southern Appalachians, on New England's hardscrabble farms, across the prairie and in the adobe villages of the Southwest, what we now call country style was once a way of life—and for some it still is. Simple, yet rich, it is a lifestyle that recalls the men and women whose hands built the homes, baked the bread, spun the wool and tended the gardens of past generations.

There is a harmony in the country style —in the way we decorate, the food we eat, the garden in our backyard and the way we spend our leisure time. That harmony is reflected in these pages.

C · H · A · P · T · E · R

1

Country Design

The beauty of the country style is its ease. It blends with anything, goes anywhere. Country accents don't clash with any other decorating style, so there can be an easy transition between your present decor and your new country decor. You don't need to redecorate overnight. The smell of fresh bread in the oven gives a country feeling to any living space just as much as a patchwork quilt on the bed.

In fact, country style is not really in the design at all, but in the feeling it conveys. You don't need ducks and spotted cows. You can create a country feeling with a simple basket of dried flowers or a pottery vase filled with fresh ones, with a pieced coverlet, a Navajo blanket, a collection of old tin and cast-iron utensils or a plain butter crock full of wooden spoons.

Country style is the everyday beauty of simple, useful things. Country style is a livable, fluid, adaptable style for any home.

If the apartment walls are not yours to accent with a stenciled border, you can achieve the same feeling by putting up stenciled muslin curtains or stacking a set of stenciled boxes on a table. If your current decorating style is far from country, start with a few easy decorative accents, then adapt or change major pieces at your leisure.

This colorful still life reflects the basic characteristics of the country style: function and simplicity. The bowls and spoons are vital for their natural beauty, but the usefulness of this collection makes it even more special.

Styles of Country Decorating

One of the joys of the country style is its diversity. No one "look" is right or wrong. Because country styles come from many different origins, they encompass several distinct design and decorating characteristics, derived from the ways in which different cultures use their native materials, tools, colors and scenery.

Your home may incorporate the elements of several different country styles instead of just one. The accent is not so much on individual ornaments or design, but on overall warmth.

Of course there are no lines to separate these styles, nor should there be. They can blend into an easy, eclectic style, where the only rules are your own taste and comfort.

© Phillip Ennis

© William Seitz

AMERICANA AND CANADIANA for a time meant painted wooden farm animals and other trendy ornaments. But, encouraged by the revived appreciation and interest in primitive art, it has now settled into a more natural, less contrived style using folk art and handmade accessories. Americana is patchwork and split oak baskets, wood and tinware, stenciling and rag rugs. It may include the use of antiques or the simple lines of wooden furniture of any period. Pottery, especially stone, spatter and scratched-ware, is at home here, as are dried weeds, old paint colors such as deep red and grayish blue, calico and Pennsylvania Dutch decorations.

© Lynn Karlin

© Phillip Ennis

© Nancy Hill/Courtesy House Beautiful Home Remodeling & Decorating

ENGLISH country style is responsible for both the original and the classic polish of Americana. From its homespun roots in the thatched crofters' cottages of the English countryside and flocks of sheep on the Yorkshire moors came most of our own traditions. The Appalachian baskets we think of as pure Americana originated on English farms, as did many herb crafts such as lavender wands and dried flower arranging. The wild beauty of the cottage garden is tempered by the sophisticated grace of the traditional English country house, with its cabbage roses, chintz and all-over florals. There is a pretty and feminine pastel grace here, where flower arrangements and floral designs give softness to the more rustic American look.

© Phillip Ennis

© Lynn Karlin

© William Seitz

© Peter Paige; Interior design by Michael Dale

SOUTHWEST style is epitomized by Santa Fe, New Mexico. This is considered by some to be the only true American style. It springs from the colors of the desert—terra cotta, ochre and intense sky blue—and its designs are definitely rooted in Native American arts and Spanish style. Stucco, adobe, raw wood, Navajo rugs and blankets, pottery, geometric designs and a solid, rugged look characterize the Southwest.

© Peter Paige; Interior design by Michael Dale

© William Seitz

© Charles S. White; Interior design by Barbara Windom

© Hoaben/FPG International

MEDITERRANEAN style brings us braids of garlic and onions, wreaths of bay leaves and brightly painted pottery. Its primary colors come from the vivid skies, seascapes, tiled roofs and poppies of the Mediterranean.

© Phillip Ennis

© William Seitz

© William Seitz

Color and Country Decorating

Just as country decorating lends itself to many different styles and combinations of styles, it also encompasses nearly any color or color scheme. While we think first of the warm, rich tones of blue milk paint, dark red, old rose and moss green, the bright primaries, russet earth tones and pastels are all equally at home in country style.

While pastels are likely to be associated with the English country style, primary colors with the Americana style, and earth tones with the Southwest, there are no firm rules. Your own eye will tell you how to mix and blend these in a way you like. With color, too, your own comfort is the key.

Color is an inexpensive way to achieve a particular style—a coat of paint can literally transform a room overnight. Color is also a good way to tie together several different styles or objects. When planning colors, choose one to predominate and use it in sixty to seventy percent of the room. That might be for wall or floor coverings, or large furniture or draperies. Then choose a secondary color which goes well with it, as well as a third accent color which might be used to tie in small decorative items.

Your color scheme might be two or three colors from one object, such as a quilt, rug or large upholstered piece, that you repeat elsewhere.

When making or choosing accents and accessories, don't feel that you must stick to the common colors. Let your imagination go free. A braided scatter rug, for example, might be cherry red and pink; a rag rug shades of rose and cranberry. Rugs are a good place to use your main colors together, since they provide a visual base for the room.

Bathrooms, because they are small, lend themselves to simple color treatments: pale rose with cream accents, or pale peach with soft green highlights.

Don't feel that everything should match—the unexpected and the uncontrived are the hallmarks of the country look that distinguish it from other, more rigid, styles.

Courtesy Levelor Lorentzen/photo: Lisanti, Decorage Studio

Adding Architectural Details

If wainscoting, chair rails, wide-board floors or paneled walls are part of your dream house, but not part of the one you live in, take heart! Many features, even rough-hewn beams, can be retrofitted.

WAINSCOTING: Simply run wide boards horizontally (for an early American look) or matched boards vertically (for a cottage-style look) right over the wall surface. Paint or stain to finish. If you want the patina of old boards, look in a barn or shed for those that have been left unfinished or have weathered.

CHAIR RAILS: To add an old-fashioned touch to a room, place chair rails on the wall at the height your chair backs hit it to protect the wall from scuffing. The easiest of all architectural details to add, these can be purchased as strips of decorative molding from a lumber store and set in place with finishing nails. Touch up the nail holes with a little wood putty and paint or stain.

WIDE-BOARD FLOORS: You can purchase new boards in a variety of widths, or you can check the attic, where floor boards are often wide *and* aged to a fine patina. Painted floors can be sanded and refinished for a natural look.

BEAMS: If your kitchen beams are not exposed, or you wish to add a free-standing beam for hanging dried flowers, herbs or old utensils, look for a fallen barn or shed and salvage suitable timber. You can buy a new beam and stain it, but it won't have the rough-hewn surface of an old one.

© William Seitz

© Bill Rothschild; Lee Napolitano Interiors

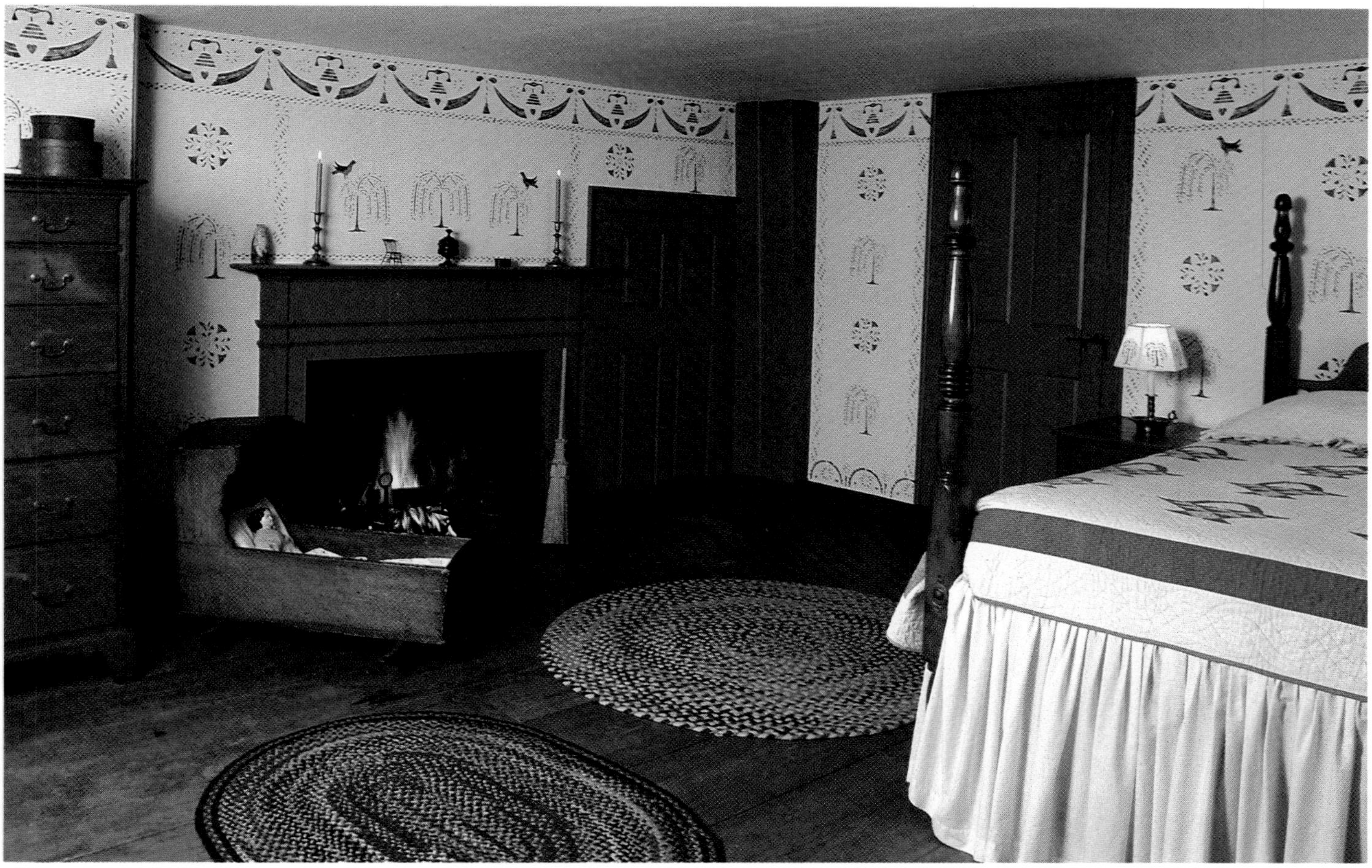

© Lynn Karlin; Sheepscot Stenciling

© Lynn Karlin/Courtesy Country Living Magazine

© William Seitz

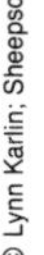

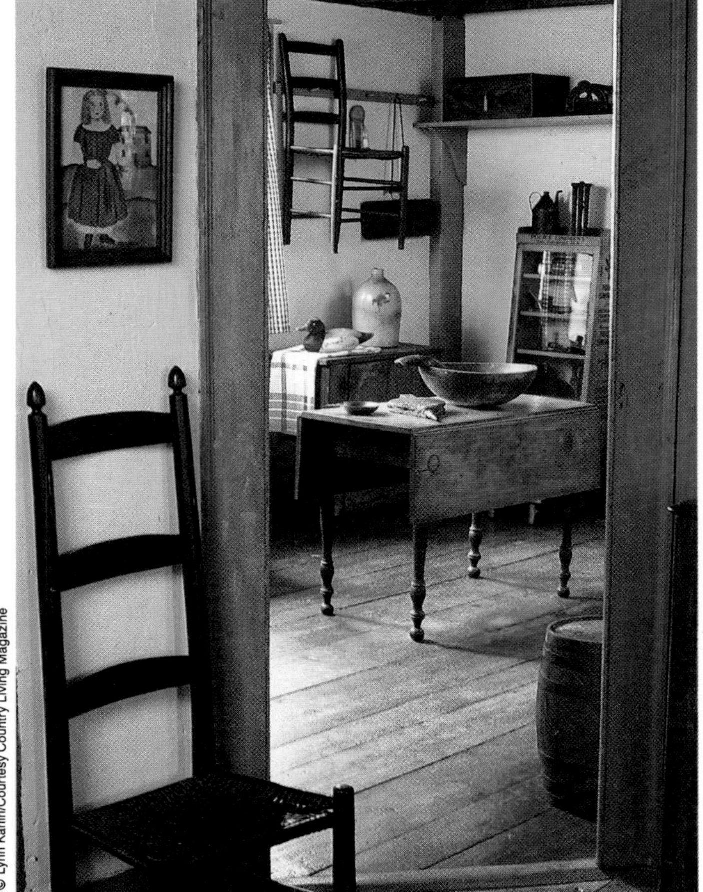

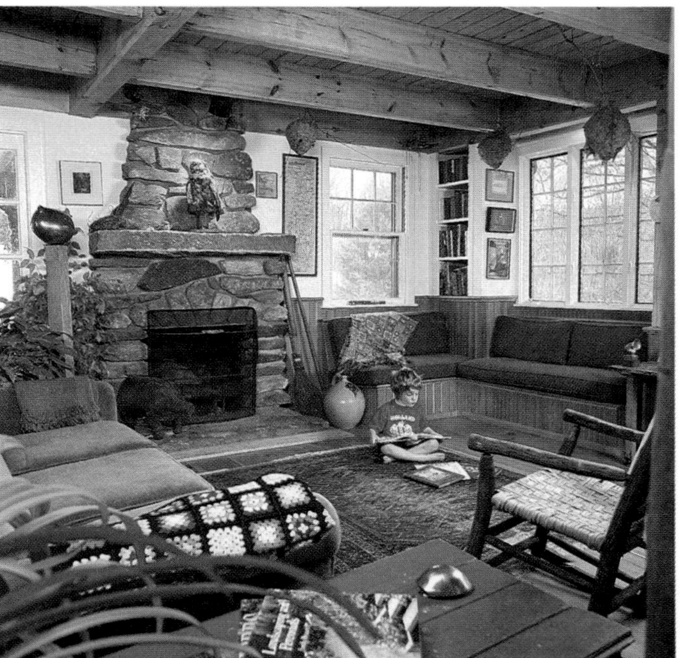

Structural details can add a country touch to any room. Here (moving clockwise from top left) are examples of wainscoting; a wide-board floor; exposed beams; a wide-board floor; a chair rail.

Wall Stencils

The appeal of stenciling is twofold: It gives a home a quintessentially country look, and it is very easy to do. Prepare the walls by painting them a neutral color (off-white is a good choice) or washing them thoroughly. Choose a stencil design that fits the room and your decorating style—you can purchase ready-cut paper stencils in formal Federal period borders, Victorian florals or traditional pineapples or leaves. Brass stencils will last longer but are harder to use if the design has small openings.

Before stenciling on your walls, practice on a piece of heavy paper. Use stiff stencil brushes, one for each color. Put a little acrylic paint onto an old dish or piece of glass and dip the stencil brush into it lightly. On a folded paper towel, wipe most of the paint from the brush until it appears almost dry. Lay the stencil on the paper and paint over the openings using an up and down, circular scrubbing motion to push the bristles onto the surface of the paper. Remember to keep the brush dry—the least little smear under the stencil means you are using too much paint. For deeper shades, go over the area several times, making sure you use the same

© Lynn Karlin; Sheepscot Stenciling

amount of paint on your brush each time.

When you can control the paint flow on your practice paper, you are ready to attach the stencil to the wall with masking tape. If you are stenciling a room with many breaks in the walls, such as doors and windows, you will need to plan your "repeat" so you don't leave off halfway through a design. Designs without a formal repeating pattern are easier to plan, as are motifs which are repeated often in a short space. You can make light pencil marks on the wall to guide your stencil placement.

For a stenciled chair rail, measure the height with a yardstick. To insure the rail is the same height all the way around the room, mark the wall with a chalk line (a string rubbed in colored chalk and snapped against the wall to leave a straight line).

Clean stencils frequently with warm water. A little rubbing alcohol on an old toothbrush is good for removing paint built up on brass stencils. Cleaning is important to keep paint from filling in the holes and making your design shrink as you work around a room. Always clean on a flat surface. Be sure to clean brushes well with soap and warm water before storing them.

Wall Coverings

Wallpaper catalogs are full of designs just right for any style of country decorating, from English chintzes and simple stencils to Williamsburg reproductions and watered silks. Ask yourself if you'll tire of looking at the pattern after too long, and avoid trendy, cute designs that will be as old as last year's hemline in a season or two.

Keep walls simple. They should serve as the background to your collections, crafts or working utensils. Nothing decorates a country room as well as the utensils that will be (or have been) used there. Let antique sewing utensils and bits of framed embroidery and patchwork decorate your sewing room. Keep a hook or two for your works-in-progress and let a half-finished sampler or the current patchwork square decorate for you.

© Phillip Ennis

© Phillip Ennis

Country Floors

Braided, hooked and rag-woven rugs are favorites for country decorating, but they certainly are not the only choices available. In a western setting or an informal room, the rich tones and bold patterns of Navajo rugs are the perfect floor covering. Stenciled floor cloths have found their way out of a century of oblivion. Easy to make and to keep clean, they can cover an entire floor or protect a heavy-wear area with a classic accent.

Plain floor boards need no covering or may be accented with runners or small throw rugs. Woven grass mats are a good choice for an entry or patio as they can be washed with a garden hose and are inexpensive to replace. These look especially nice as a counterpoint to bright Mexican or Native American textiles.

Commercial floor coverings come in a variety of styles, suggesting Mediterranean country tiles, stones, brick and other surfaces. These are easy to care for and stand up well in work and heavily trafficked areas such as the kitchen. Real tile is the best choice for entry areas and under wood stoves, where it is not only the safest floor covering, but looks right at home. For outdoor surfaces, choose brick; indoors, use brick only for hearths, entries and wood stove bases.

A Gallery Of Floor Coverings

RAG RUGS: Woven of scrap fabric on a string weft, these are usually narrow, often made as runners for hallways and stairs. Machine-made rugs in this style are inexpensive and readily available in solids and tweeds. Early rag rugs were woven of random tweeds.

BRAIDED RUGS: Plaited of woolen fabrics stitched in a spiral, braided rugs come in many sizes. They may be all-over tweeds or braided in bands of separate colors. Machine-made imitations are available, but don't look like the real thing. (To make your own braided rug see page 28.)

FLOOR CLOTHS: The forerunner of linoleum squares, these are made of heavy canvas or duck, painted for durability and decoration and often stenciled. Almost a lost art, floor cloths are again being made professionally.

Courtesy Williams-Sonoma

© Bill Rothschild; Pat McMillan Interiors

© William Seitz

NAVAJO RUGS: Woven of fine wool in a tight weave that covers the warp threads, Navajo rugs are among the most sought-after Native American crafts. Bold geometric designs in bright primary and earth colors characterize the style. Other woven rugs, such as those made in Mexico and South America, are also popular and come in a wide variety of designs and colors.

ORIENTALS: There is a great variety of Oriental rugs and each region of the Orient has developed its own unique colors, designs and techniques. Grouped with fine antiques in a formal setting, they blend well in country decorating. They are popular for dining rooms and as small throw rugs in any setting. Fine, handmade wool Orientals are among the world's most costly floor coverings, but machine-made carpets in the same characteristic styles, colors and patterns are available in all price ranges.

HOOKED RUGS: Very thin strips of wool fabric are pulled into loops through a burlap base. Worked on a frame, hooked rugs may be any size or shape.

Rugs add warmth to any country room. Here is an oriental rug in a country dining room; a braided rug in a blue bedroom; and a Navajo rug in a distinctively Southwestern home.

Braiding A Rug

If you can braid pigtails, you can braid a rug. No floor covering brings more warmth to a country setting, none requires simpler materials and tools—no loom, no frame, no special hooks—and you don't have to wait until it's finished to use it.

Start by collecting wool scraps—a thorough closet cleaning usually turns up enough for a start. Be sure the fabric is wool, not synthetic, which wears unevenly. Progress from your closets to those of your friends, then to thrift shops and yard sales. When all else fails, or to get special colors, you can buy wool scraps by the pound from mill stores.

Take the garments apart, removing the buttons, zippers and hems, and wash the fabric well in warm, sudsy water. Rinse it well and dry it. This cleans, shrinks and fluffs the fabric. Cut the fabric into strips along the straight of the fabric (never on a bias) according to the thickness you want for the finished braid. Cut thick fabrics narrower and flannels wider so they will be even when rolled for braiding.

Sort the fabric by color and roll it up to keep it flat. Once you have the fabric assembled, you can plan the design of the rug and decide what colors you will need to buy for accent or fillers. You will need about two-thirds of a pound of wool for each square foot of finished rug. (If you have to buy wool, this is about one yard of fifty-four-inch fabric.)

In planning the color combination, think of the room the rug will be in. If you wish to have one color dominate, plan to use several rows of it together in a solid bank about halfway through the rug. Blend it in by using one strand of it with two of the neighboring color, then two of it and one of the other, then the solid bank. Blend it out by reversing this order. It is a good idea to do this when changing colors to keep your rug harmonious.

Braiding is quite easy. Begin by joining two of the first three strands by cutting and stitching on a bias. This is because a straight cut would make a very lumpy seam; cutting on a bias spreads the thickness out. Join the third strand at a right angle to form a "T." Fold the raw edges of each piece inside and begin braiding. As soon as you have enough braid, close the end into a drawer or clamp it in a clipboard to hold it firm as you work. Continue to fold the raw edges inside each strip as you braid. If you keep the seams to the right on all the strips as you braid, these will be stitched into a seam in the finished rug, making it completely reversible.

Keep the braid tight enough so that the eraser end of a pencil cannot be forced through the spaces. When you reach the end of a wool strip, cut it on a bias and attach a new piece as you did at the beginning. Be sure the seam faces inside the braid.

Before you begin to braid you must decide how long to make the center braid. This determines the difference between the length and the width of the finished rug. The center braid is first made twice the desired length, then doubled over and laced together. The rest of the rug is laced onto this center, continuing in a clockwise spiral.

Lace the braids together with a blunt needle and stout thread, pushing the needle through the spaces in the braid, not through the fabric, and working from the underside. Lace on a flat surface, placing the braids so that they fit perfectly. The loops on one braid should fit into the dents of the other. You will have to skip a loop or two when turning the corners.

Your rug will take shape very quickly, and as it begins to look like a rug, you will gain confidence. The braid should be laced onto the rug firmly, but not stretched tightly around it. Be careful to keep the rug flat and redo any lacing that causes a pucker (or you will have a bowl-shaped rug). When the rug is the size you want, narrow the strips to form a tapered braid at a corner, where it won't show as much, and lace into place, tucking the last little point into the braid.

Pierced Tin Cabinets

Pierced tin can add a unique, relaxed country charm to a kitchen or dining room. The technique was originally used for pie safes, because it let air circulate around the pie but kept the flies out. The tinwork was often homemade, since it was easy to make.

You can use the same process to make your own pierced tin cabinets. All you need are an awl or ice pick, a flat 1/4-inch chisel, a mallet and a short board.

First, draw your pattern on paper. (A rough outline of the design is enough.) Traditional designs are based on a geometric diamond, sunburst or oval shape. You can copy the design from an old tin panel, if you have one. Just put a piece of white paper over the panel and then rub a black crayon over the pattern. Whether you draw your own pattern or trace it, be sure to leave a 1-inch border all the way around the design.

Place a sheet of tin on the board and tape the pattern in place. Following the lines of the design, punch holes by placing the awl or chisel at right angles to the tin and striking it with the mallet. Keep the blows even to assure even-sized holes. These should be spaced close enough together to form a distinct pattern but not so close that they cause the tin to split. Dots and slits almost always run in rows, not random patterns. Use small crosses and sunbursts to fill bare spaces.

Tin panels may be put in existing cabinet doors if the edge frame is strong enough to stand alone and the center panel can be removed. Simply glue or tack the tin into the hole left by the panel. The rough side of the tin should face outward so you won't scratch your hand as you reach in.

If you are building new cabinets, you can design your doors for the panels. Make the doors as you would a picture frame, with 2- to 3-inch-wide sides and 4- to 5-inch-wide tops and bottoms. The molding design should be fairly plain to fit in with the country simplicity of the tin.

There are certain decorating details to remember if you are using pierced tin. It will be the focal point of any room in which it is used extensively. Other metal work, such as hinges or knobs, will either detract from the tin or give the room a "busy" look. Choose invisible hinges and white porcelain knobs, which will complement the tin color.

Caring for the tin is quite easy. Since its only enemy is rust, clean it with mild soap and a damp cloth. Dry it well and give it a light rubbing of vegetable oil to protect the finish from moisture.

Finding the Right Furniture

You don't need antiques to give your home a warm country feeling. Although a set of priceless arrow-back Windsor chairs would be nice to have around your kitchen table, a set of pressed backed chairs from a flea market can be just as comfortable. Less expensive and even more interesting would be a series of unmatched chairs, each with its own style.

Collecting chairs at junk shops and flea markets can be fun, and you can use unmatched chairs until you find several of a similar style. Many of these odd chairs will be painted, and it may surprise you to learn that many were painted when they were made, to disguise the many different woods used. Pine was easier to shape into plank seats, while harder woods took well to turning for rungs. Legs might be yet a third type of wood. Painting solved the problem for early cabinet-makers just as it can for you.

Chairs of little distinction can become attractive and inviting after a coat of paint turns them a rich, warm color and braided mats cover their seats.

Flat surfaces such as tables and bureaus are easier to strip and refinish than turned furniture. Spool furniture is the hardest to strip, which is why you'll often find that it's covered with several layers of paint.

But don't be too quick to strip. Many pieces, especially those in the cottage style, were originally false-grained or painted, and you may be able to restore these classic decorative finishes. Even a damaged painted design or false-grained finish has more charm than a refinished piece. Of course, you would never strip a fine antique yourself—that is a job for an expert restorer.

© Bill Rothschild; Martin Kuckley & Associates

© Bill Rothschild; Classic Galleries

© William Seitz

Furniture Styles

FINE ANTIQUES include those from the Hepplewhite, Queen Anne, William and Mary, Chippendale, Sheraton and other formal styles. These are handmade, cabinetmaker pieces for the serious collector.

COTTAGE furniture is characterized by extensive spool turning, colored designs (usually floral) painted over false graining and other decorations. Most often found in bedroom furniture such as beds, chests, night stands and towel racks.

MISSION was the first mass-produced furniture style, and it is popular with country decorators for its clean lines and the golden oak wood most often used. Mission is particularly suited to the Southwestern style.

VICTORIAN furniture is heavily carved and upholstered, most often made of dark woods. Although pieces from this era evoke a definite style of their own, they can be mixed with simpler country styles to add character to a room.

FRENCH CANADIAN furniture is prevalent in Quebec, where traditional French furniture designs were adapted by the colonists. Simple joined chests, benches, stools and chairs are common. They are often made of pine, although walnut and butternut woods are used for heavier pieces.

SHAKER furniture's clean, simple lines are among the most sought-after for country decorating. Reproductions are available, especially at restored Shaker villages where contemporary craftsmen work in the Shaker shops.

© Bill Rothschild; Classic Galleries

© Phillip Ennis

© Myrleen Ferguson/PhotoEdit

A Primer of Furniture Finishes

PAINT: Fast and easy. Use it to cover repairs, unmatched woods or an undistinguished piece. Paint stores carry a variety of colors; check directions on cans for furniture use.

EURETHANE: Easy to use, shows wood grain well. Comes in gloss or matte finish. Quick drying, durable finish. Follow directions on can.

HAND RUBBED: This time-consuming process for better pieces involves alternating shellac cut with alcohol and hand-rubbing with oil. Another process uses only repeated coats of rubbed tung oil wiped clean between coats. Brings out the beauty of richly grained woods.

FALSE GRAINED: Uses one solid coat of paint followed by a stippled or streaked coat to simulate wood grain. Very popular late Victorian technique, quite easy to do.

ORIGINAL: The easiest of all. Leave furniture in its found state, complete with worn areas, distresses and checked finish. A good washing with Murphy's Oil Soap and a coat of wax will clean and protect the surface.

Country furniture styles include (opposite page, top to bottom) fine antiques and cottage; and Shaker (this page).

Wood Stoves

A wood stove in the kitchen is more than a cooking surface and a source of heat. It is the sizzle and steamy fragrance of woolen mittens drying, the toasty feel of warmed boots on a cold morning, the welcoming aroma of apple pie hot out of the oven just as the school bus stops at the mailbox. It is the heart and soul of a country home.

Using a wood stove is mostly a matter of common sense. If you remember that a fire requires oxygen, that smoke rises, and that small wood burns faster, you will be able to build and maintain a good fire.

The dampers (the vents that allow air into stoves and chimneys) vary from stove to stove, but most have one beside the firebox (the place where the fire is), one on the back of the top above the oven and one on the stovepipe near the wall. The trick is to adjust these during each part of the process so the fire gets enough air to burn without letting all the heat go up the chimney.

To start a fire, open all three dampers as far as possible. Put three or four sheets of crumpled newspaper into the firebox, then a few sticks of the thin-split kindling, then two larger pieces of wood, also split. Don't stack these solid, but angle them enough so air can circulate between them. Light the paper with a match and close the door. The fire should be burning merrily in a few minutes, after which you can open the door and add some larger pieces of wood.

© Bill Rothschild; Barbara Fox Interiors

Wood Stove Safety

A wood stove in your home presents certain problems not associated with an electric or gas range, and it is essential that you consider these before installing one. First, it must never be set on a wood floor. Brick, tile, stone or another fire-resistant surface must be under it and extend out several inches on all sides. Failing this, an insulated metal "stove board" can be used to separate it from the floor.

The wall behind the stove should also be brick or stone, or the stove should sit at least 24 inches from the wall. The area where the stovepipe connects to the chimney should be fireproof; any portion of the stove or pipe should be at least 18 inches from an unprotected surface.

Since each area has its own regulations, it is best to call your local fire chief or your insurance company for exact specifications.

Be sure to inspect your chimney and stovepipe regularly for creosote, which causes chimney fires, and clean them whenever there is a buildup. Always check chimneys before their first use in the fall to be sure they haven't become home to birds over the summer.

© Lynn Karlin

Never feed a fire through the top of the stove—it is dangerous and allows smoke to escape into the room. When the fire is burning well, close the dampers, always starting from the bottom and working up. You will soon learn how to regulate these to give you the heat you want. To prevent smoking, close the the bottom damper and open the chimney damper a little more. *For safety, the bottom damper should never be open unless the chimney damper also is open.*

To cook on the stove, you move the cooking pan and adjust the damper instead of turning a dial. And when cooking on a wood stove remember that the surface above the woodbox is the hottest, over the oven is cooler.

Old Wood Stove Utensils For Cooks and Collectors

Most wood stove utensils are made of good, sturdy cast iron. It conducts heat evenly, is heavy enough to withstand direct flame, and doesn't warp. Because wood stove plates are standard, many fit right in when a stove lid is removed.

GRIDDLE: An oval, flat pan with a small rim and handles at each end. It fits into the space left by the removal of two lids and the connector. It works well for pancakes, grilled sandwiches, French toast or anything else that needs a large frying surface. It also doubles as a perfect comal for tortillas.

WAFFLE IRON: An ingenious round frame that sits in a burner hole to hold a round iron which flips over to cook the waffle on both sides. There are several different styles of these irons, and they all make perfect waffles as long as they are seasoned well with oil.

DOUGHNUT KETTLE: A semi-spherical cast-iron pot that fits directly into a stove-lid hole. Heat is distributed directly and evenly to keep fat at a fairly even temperature.

JOHNNYCAKE PAN: An oval griddle with four hinged, round lids. Some flip over entirely inside a frame, like the waffle iron. These pans are hard to find, but they're among the most interesting utensils.

Caring for Cast Iron

New cast iron needs seasoning before it is used, or everything will stick to it. To do this, rub the cast iron heavily with vegetable oil and bake it for an hour at 200°F. Let it cool slowly in the oven, then wipe out excess oil.

The same method is used to restore old cast iron that is dirty or rusty. Scour it thoroughly, removing the rust with steel wool. Dry it well and warm slightly over a stove burner to be sure there is no moisture remaining. Then follow the directions for seasoning. If it has taken a lot of scouring, you may have to bake it longer and add more oil before it is ready to use.

Cooking With a Wood Stove

Heat is heat, and a 350°F oven is a 350°F oven, whether it is in a big black wood stove or a shiny new electric range. So there is no reason why bread should taste better baked in a wood stove, but it does. Bread is also the easiest thing for a new wood stove cook to try, since it is forgiving and can withstand irregular and uneven temperatures. It may get a little crusty or brown on one side, but it will still be delicious.

You should do a little homework before using your wood stove, because they don't come with owners' manuals. Check its heat with a thermometer and see if the dial on the door is correct. If it isn't, you need to know how far off it is and in which direction, or you will have to use an inside thermometer regularly. Be sure the oven damper is in the right position to let air circulate around it. The fire should be going well ahead of time.

Hardwood is the best for baking because it burns hot, slowly and evenly. It also makes a good bed of coals which helps keep the oven temperature even.

This wood stove holds a variety of utensils, including a waffle iron, in the lower-right-hand corner.

White Bread

4 c. lukewarm milk
3/4 c. sugar
4 tsp. salt
1/4 c. vegetable oil
2 pkgs dry yeast, dissolved in 1/2 c. lukewarm water
12 c. flour

Combine the sugar, salt and oil with the warm milk and add the yeast. Stir in the flour slowly, one cup at a time, until the dough is stiff. Turn the dough out onto a well-floured board and knead for 15 minutes, adding remaining flour to the board as necessary.

Place the ball of dough in a large, greased bowl, cover with a towel and let it rise on the warming shelf of your stove until doubled (usually a little more than an hour). Punch down with a floured fist, cover and let it rise again. Punch it down, divide into fourths and shape into loaves. Place these in greased pans and let them rise.

Bake in a 350°F oven for 45 minutes or until the bread feels crisp and hollow when you tap it with your finger. While they are baking, move the loaves around twice to make sure they all bake evenly.

Makes 4 loaves. Just cut the ingredients in half to make 2 loaves.

Wood Stove Potpourri

whole cloves
whole allspice
stick cinnamon
chopped, dried orange peel

Mix together equal amounts of the above ingredients. You can store this mixture in an open jar as a potpourri until you need it. To use it, place a tablespoonful of potpourri in a saucepan of water on the back of the wood stove to simmer. Be sure to add water as it boils away.

Baked Beans

2 lb. dry kidney beans
1/2 lb. salt pork
3/4 c. molasses
1 large onion
2 qt. water
2 tsp. salt
1 tsp. dry mustard

Baked beans are a classic New England food. They go well with many country meals. Preheat oven to 200°F. In a large saucepan, wash the beans, cover them with water and boil for 5 minutes. Let them stand off the stove for an hour. Return them to the stove and cook slowly until skins begin to break. Drain the bean water into another saucepan and soak the salt pork for 15 minutes in this hot cooking liquid. Remove pork and score it in several places.

Place the beans, pork and remaining ingredients into a bean pot, adding one cup of the water in which the beans and salt pork have soaked. Stir well and add enough water to cover the beans. Cover the pot and bake for 8 hours. Check and add more water if needed.

Serves 8 to 10.

Cornmeal Pancakes

3/4 c. water
1/4 c. stone-ground cornmeal
3/4 c. sour milk or buttermilk
2 tbsp. sugar
1/2 tsp. baking powder
1 c. flour
1/2 tsp. salt
1 egg, beaten
2 tbsp. vegetable oil

Put the water in a saucepan and bring to a good, rolling boil. Sprinkle in the cornmeal and cook for 3 to 4 minutes, stirring constantly. Remove from heat and stir in the sour milk. Sift dry ingredients and add, alternating between them, the egg and the oil. Pour onto a hot griddle, spreading with a spatula if necessary. Bake and flip when nicely browned.

Makes approximately 12 medium-size pancakes.

© Lynn Karlin

The Hearth of the Matter: Using A Fireplace

The warm glow of a fireplace will never go out of style. Even when it lost its original purpose as a place to cook and a source of heat, the fireplace stayed on.

The greatest temptation when using a fireplace is to build a Fourth of July bonfire in it. But a small fire will toast your toes, roast chestnuts and pop corn (and even cook your stew for dinner if you have a crane and a pot) far better than a large one.

Although there are many fireplace accessories available, all you really need are andirons or a fire grate, a screen and a pair of long-handled tongs. Andirons are more than just decoration—they hold the wood up off the hearth, allowing air to circulate under the fire and keep it burning. The screen protects both you and your room from flying embers, and the tongs save a lot of burned fingers.

To build a fire, begin with fire-starters or a few sheets of tightly twisted newspaper laid on the hearth between the andirons or under the grate.

© Lynn Karlin

© Lynn Karlin

Above these lay several pieces of split kindling, followed by two or three small split logs. Be sure the damper is wide open and light the starters or newspaper.

After the kindling is burning well and the larger pieces have caught, you may want to add a little more wood. Always keep the screen in front of the fire when you are not actually working with it.

Fireplaces are good for roasting and broiling; use a long-handled grill which you can either hold or prop over the hot coals. Special pans are made for roasting chestnuts, which is a delightful family activity. You can also pop corn, or roast sausages on long forks over the fire.

Reflector ovens are fun to use in front of the fire, where they take advantage of the fireplace's own reflective qualities. These can be used to roast chicken or bake biscuits. The best fires for this are built fairly low and against a good-sized backlog which reflects the heat into the oven. To check the progress of food, simply turn the entire oven around and look inside.

Fireplaces may not be the most efficient way to heat rooms, but their charm as a cheerful focal point and family gathering place will always assure them a place in the country home.

© Lynn Karlin

© Bart Barlow/Envision

© Anita Sabarese

© Jerry Howard/Positive Images

The Well-tempered Wood Pile

Whether for the stove or the fireplace, the characteristics of a good wood pile are the same. It should contain a variety of hardwoods, with as much softwood as is needed for kindling.

The first thing to know about wood is which kinds burn best. There are two criteria for this: how hot it burns; and how well it burns. Some woods, like cherry, burn hot enough, but they sputter and spit too much for a fireplace. Others, like poplar and aspen, burn fast, but smell terrible.

The best woods include beech, sugar maple, red and white oak, yellow and black birch, hickory, apple and pear. Elm, willow and pine will fill your chimney with dangerous creosote.

Stacking wood is a matter of art and energy. To some, a perfectly stacked wood pile is like a well mowed lawn—it's a social necessity. The wood really doesn't care, as long as it is off the ground a little, has good air circulation and is protected from rain and snow. Some people stack by size, while others prefer to mix sizes so that even when gathered in the dark, an armful will provide a good mix of woods.

© Lynn Karlin

C · H · A · P · T · E · R

2

Country Collections

While it isn't necessary to collect only one specific type of item, many people find that looking for a particular object makes browsing in antique shops, flea markets and yard sales more fun. For others, collecting means looking for things that are different in nature and use, but are tied together by a decorating theme. Thus, furniture, kitchen utensils, crockery, baskets, rag rugs and a rocking horse could all be part of a collection.

Some enjoy the challenge of very specific collections. Instead of looking for old toys they collect children's blocks; instead of tools they collect old block planes. Let your own interests be your guide to collecting. A cook may enjoy finding obsolete kitchen implements such as a cork-sizer, meat juice extractor or cream separator. Or they may limit the scope and try to find as many kinds of nutmeg graters as possible. A gardener may look for herb-related antiques or old farm implements. Someone who likes to sew may collect a number of sewing basket items, or only pincushions.

If nothing else, collecting a particular item gives you something to reply to the antique dealer who asks if you are looking for something special.

Country collections are often very eclectic, because the country style can accommodate a lot of different designs. The collection here includes a duck, an elephant, cinnamon sticks, a wooden box, an antique table, a woven rug and a basket. And despite their differences, together they give a unified country look.

© Louis Sahuc/Stock Options

Where to Find Antiques

There are many different sources of nice old country pieces and each has its own set of customers and its own advantages. The best source, of course is to inherit a barnfull, but lacking that, these are the best.

© Nancy A. Butler/FPG International

ANTIQUE SHOPS: These vary greatly, but are usually among the most expensive sources. Look for shops away from heavily traveled routes and tourist destinations, and keep at least a mental record of the price range of items you are interested in.

ANTIQUE SHOWS: Dealers bring items to display at shows alongside other dealers. You will find a wide variety of antiques, and have a chance to compare many prices under one roof. Most dealers bring smaller pieces and collectibles to shows, but you may also find furniture and larger things as well. Early morning is the best time for rare items, late afternoon for bargaining.

ANTIQUE MALLS: These are permanent antique shows, where a number of dealers have spaces under one roof. Small malls have separate shops where each dealer sells his own merchandise, while others work on a cooperative basis with many displays and a central check out. With the latter, you won't have much luck with bargaining.

AUCTIONS: If you can resist the excitement that sometimes takes over when the bidding is fast, auctions are an excellent place to find country antiques. The best are on-site house auctions, where they often bring out boxes full of unsorted treasures late in the day.

FLEA MARKETS: A lot less formal than antique shows, these are often held out-of-doors and you usually have to walk past a lot of second-hand and new items to find the treasures. But if you go early, you can find some bargains, especially if you are looking for something that is not a current collecting craze.

YARD SALES: You have to get to these before the antique dealers do, especially if it's a real "attic cleaning" or moving sale where long forgotten objects may be uncovered and offered for sale by people who do not follow the antiques market. You may have to look for a long time, but you can find some surprising gems.

Shopping for Country Crafts

The decorations and furnishings for a country home need not be antiques. The charm of the country style is that it is the perfect showcase for handcrafted or one-of-a-kind pieces, old or new. There are several good sources of fine handicrafts.

© Robert Perron

© Robert Perron

ARTISANS' COOPERATIVES: Shops run by art associations or cooperatives offer a wide selection of crafts, often at lower prices than gift shops. The advantage, too, is that everything you find in a cooperative is handmade, whereas gift shops tend to mix the machine-manufactured with authentic handicrafts. Although gift shops may offer some excellent imported items that are attractive and will serve your purpose well, you do want to know if you are really buying handcrafted originals.

© Robert Perron

Craft Studios: These are usually the best places to shop for larger items and those that need to be specially ordered, such as quilts or handmade rugs. You can watch the craftsman work, see samples in progress and discuss your special needs. Nothing beats dealing directly with the craftsman. But studios are often widely separated and off the beaten path. When you are traveling, ask the local tourist office if they have a map or listing of craft studios in the area. Many chambers of commerce and tourist offices publish craft guides and you can quickly check to see if there are any that interest you along your route of travel.

© Jerry Howard/Positive Images

© Jerry Howard/Positive Images

Craft Shows: While these shows vary greatly in size, quality and style, they are still a very good place for you to meet craftsmen and see their work. Choose a large, well established show or one that is run by an arts or crafts organization. Your local arts council can suggest shows in your area.

This type of show might have quilters, with both original designs and traditional patterns, basket makers, weavers, potters, woodworkers, blacksmiths and more.

How To Shop

At most flea markets, yard sales and even with antique dealers, bargaining is standard practice. Larger or metropolitan galleries may have fixed prices, but most others are flexible. How you bargain depends on your attitude. Usually the simple question, "Is this the best price you can give me on this?" will tell you whether there is any room for negotiation.

Another less direct way is to indicate your interest in something, hesitate and move on to look at other things, then return to look at the first item again. A dealer who is willing to bargain will usually suggest a better price at this point.

Depending on how much time you have, it is often better to poke about and see what's there before asking for an item you seek. If you enter a shop or booth and ask for nutmeg graters, you are immediately placing yourself at a disadvantage in bargaining. But before you leave a shop it is wise to ask, since the owner may have things that are not on display.

Displaying Country Collections

By their very nature, country collections take well to informal displays. These treasures are at home hung from rafters, stacked in corners or arranged in display cabinets made from old store crates.

In addition, many favorite pieces of country furniture are perfect showcases. Hutches, old post office mail cabinets, spice chests, pie safes, quilt racks, thread cabinets, ice boxes, type trays, store crates, round Shaker boxes, baskets, coatracks and silverware trays are all good containers for collections, along with being collectibles themselves.

Crates can be stacked or, if they are fairly shallow, can be hung on the wall to create an informal set of shelves. Type trays are perfect shadow-box shelves for a collection of miniatures, thimbles or a mixture of small objects. Display old linens or keep new ones within handy reach with quilt racks; they also make perfect towel racks in a guest room or bath.

© Lynn Karlin/Courtesy Country Living Magazine

© Lynn Karlin/Courtesy Country Living Magazine

Mail cabinets are just right for displaying a collection of small kitchen utensils or old toys. Since many kitchen pieces were designed to hang, these can also be shown beautifully against a wooden or plaster wall or along the end of a kitchen cabinet. A beam is a good place to hang larger utensils, baskets, cast iron or graniteware.

Since many country collectibles (such as containers) also are useful pieces in their own right, you can use them as originally intended and decorate your home at the same time. Old tins or glass-topped canning jars make attractive containers for storing dry ingredients in the kitchen or pantry; crocks hold wooden spoons; baskets hold rolled kitchen or bathroom towels; and wooden boxes store soaps and cosmetics. Stack old wooden boxes and wicker baskets on open shelves. All of these items can earn their keep while adding a country flavor to your home.

© Nancy Hill

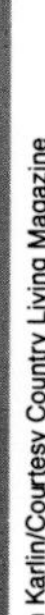
© Lynn Karlin/Courtesy Country Living Magazine

Quilts

No single household item bespeaks the North American country style quite as eloquently as a patchwork quilt. Quilts are the quintessence of American folk art, born of our ethic and way of life.

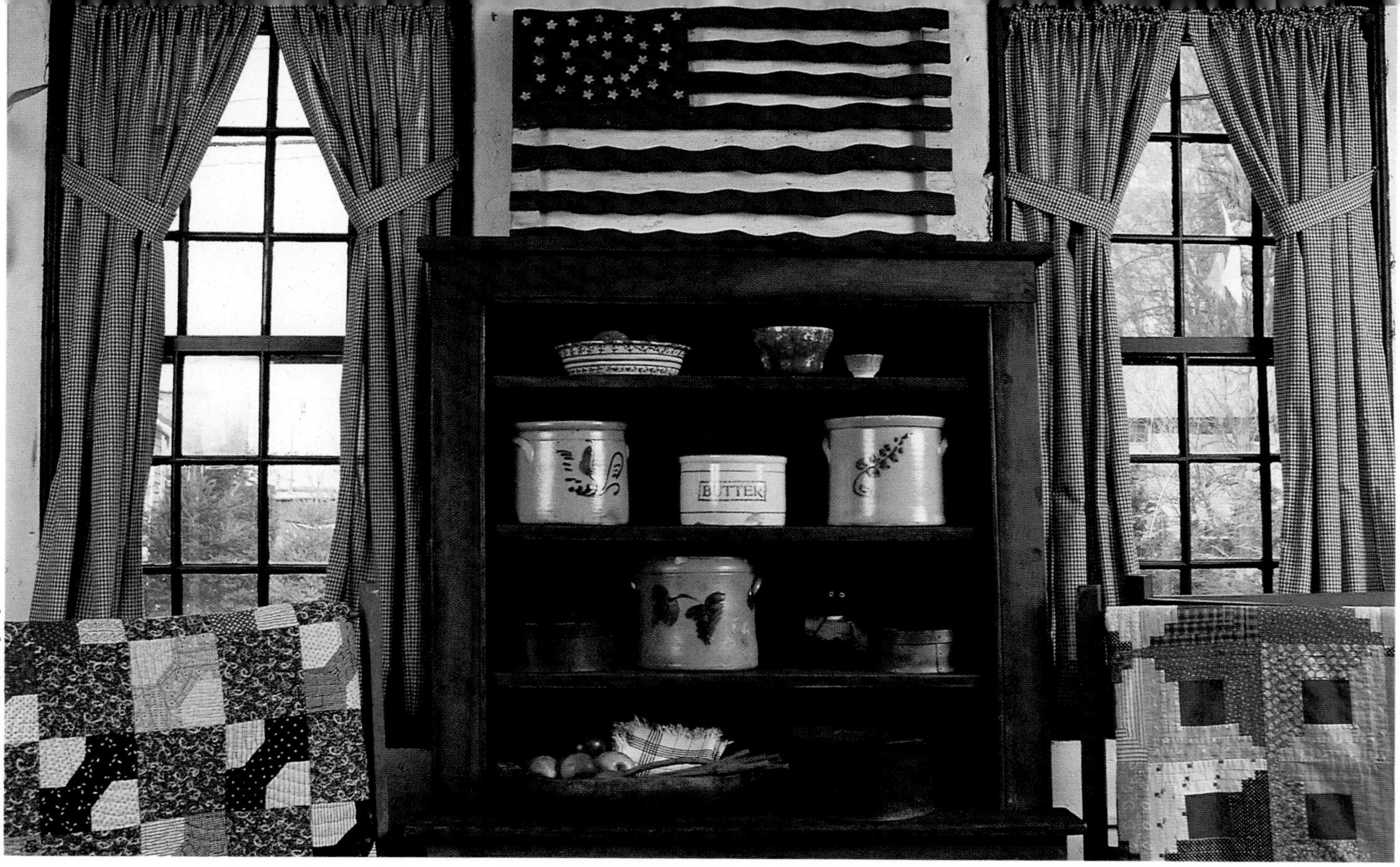

© Lynn Karlin/Courtesy Country Living Magazine

© Dave Bartruff/FPG International

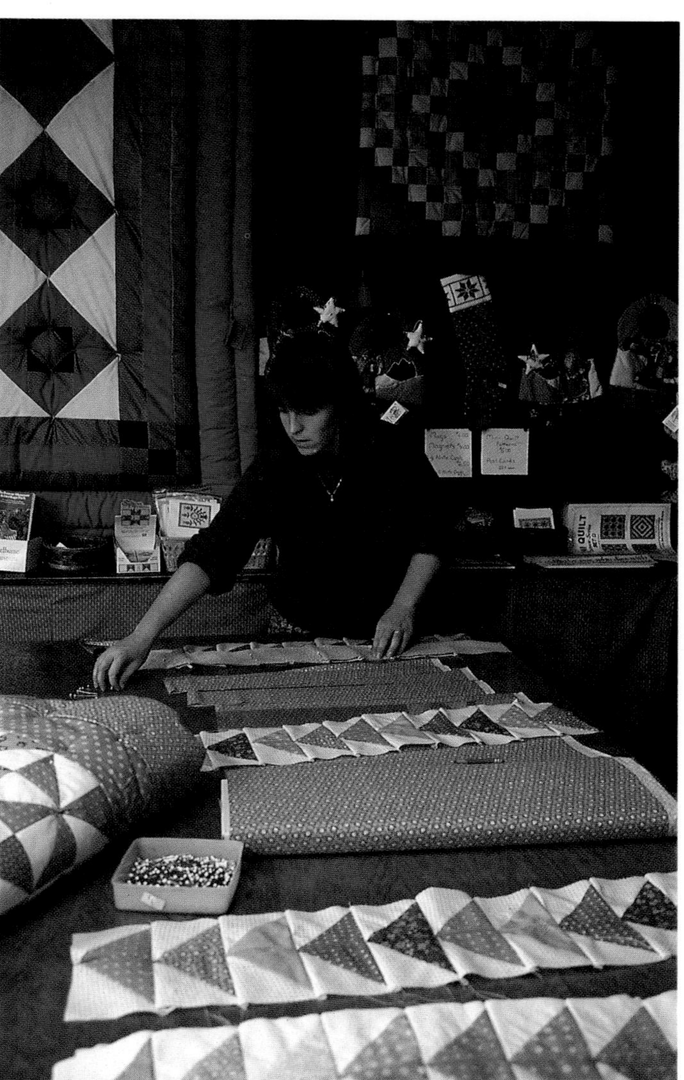

Caring for Quilts

Whether you have a treasured old quilt or one you've made yourself and hope will someday become an heirloom, you will want to take the best possible care of it.

First check the construction of the quilt and the fiber of the top, batting and backing. Look for loose or broken stitches, damaged embroidery or frayed fabric.

The best way to repair old quilts is to cover the damaged area with sheer fabric that will hold it together and prevent more pulling and tearing, but still allow the design to show through. Baste it in place with cotton thread, using tacked ends instead of knots, which could rip through the fabric. If you do other repair work, such as fixing an area of severe wear, use fabrics that are in keeping with the original and work over the damaged area without cutting it away. You can appliqué even irregular shapes right over damaged areas with blind stitching.

Storing quilts improperly can cause severe damage. They should be stored in the living area, not in the attic or basement, where variations in the humidity and temperature could ruin the fabric. Folding puts a strain on both the stitching and the fabric. If a quilt must be folded, vary the folds each time and pad the insides of the folds with crumpled tissue paper to avoid creases.

The best storage method is to roll the quilt around a tube at least 3 inches in diameter, top side in, and wrap it in tissue paper or cotton fabric. Lay the tube horizontally on a shelf or suspend it on wall brackets in a dark, ventilated area.

© Anita Sabarese

Potpourri: The Sweet Smell of Country

Nothing evokes a memory quite like fragrance—the sultry smell of a pine forest on a hot summer day, the aroma of apple pie in the oven, the scent of wreaths and Christmas trees.

When these fragrances and others are out of season, you can bring them back if you've captured them in potpourri. It's surprisingly easy.

The first step in making potpourri, unless you plan to purchase all your ingredients, is saving and drying the flowers, herbs and leaves as they come into bloom.

Roses, lavender, chamomile, orange blossom, lemon, marigold, jasmine, lime flowers and scented geraniums are all wonderfully fragrant when dried. Herbs such as mint, lemon balm, lemon verbena, tansy, bergamot and sweetfern are also highly fragrant. Strawflowers, statice, delphinium, celosia, marigolds, zinnias, baby's breath, calendula, even tulips and daffodils, will add both color and bulk.

To dry plants with long stems, tie them into bundles and hang them upside down in an airy, shady place. Hanging them inside a paper bag will keep them clean and prevent the loss of little pieces. To dry small flowers or single blossoms, lay them on a screen in a shady place until they are crisp, then store them in bags or jars.

Non-gardeners will be pleased to learn that wonderful potpourris can be blended in the kitchen from ingredients right off the shelf. Mix a potpourri of cinnamon sticks, whole cloves, allspice, thyme, rosemary, mint, marjoram, and bay leaves, alone or blended with flowers. Be sure to save all your orange, lemon, lime and tangerine peels, which can be cut into strips and dried to add a piquant touch to spice or floral potpourris.

While scent is the most important consideration, it is not the only one. If you want to display the blend in a glass jar or open container, include brightly colored blossoms to make the potpourri as beautiful as it is aromatic.

Once a potpourri smells and looks good, it is time to consider preserving and strengthening its scent. Orris, the dried root of the florentine iris, is the best fixative, and should be used chipped, not powdered. It has no scent of its own, but helps preserve others.

Since drying evaporates some of the fragrant oils in the flowers, it is wise to replace these with essential oils. Rose is the most versatile of these, blending well with nearly any other fragrance.

© Robert Perron

Lavender is the strongest and tends to dominate others. Bay, balsam, cedar, orange, lemon, gardenia and carnation are other favorites.

Simply mix your ingredients in whatever quantity you have or like, and add one or two tablespoons of orris root per pint. Use four to eight drops of the essential oil to a pint. Mix well and seal in a jar with plenty of air space. Shake or stir it daily for two weeks to allow it to blend and ripen. After that, your potpourri is ready to put in a bowl and enjoy.

To preserve the life of potpourri, keep it covered as many hours a day as it is open. Many people close the jar or cover the dish at night, opening it each morning. Try to keep the blend out of the sun, which will fade both the color and scent. If the mixture loses its fragrance, simply treat it as you would a brand new mix—add orris root and oil and let it blend in a large jar for two weeks.

© Robert Perron

© Robert Perron

Summer Garden Potpourri

1/2 c. pink roses
1/2 c. thyme
1/4 c. lemon verbena
1/4 c. rosemary
1/4 c. lavender
1/2 c. mixed blossoms
8 bay leaves
1 tbsp. whole cloves
2 tbsp. orris root
3 drops each rose and bay oils
1 drop lavender oil

Autumn Woods Potpourri

1/4 c. cedar shavings
1/4 c. soft stick cinnamon
1/4 c. balsam needles
1/4 c. calendula
1/4 c. lemon verbena
1/4 c. eucalyptus leaves
10 bay leaves
2 tbsp. orris root
4 drops each bay, balsam and cedar oil

Herb Dryer

This classically simple rack for drying bunches of herbs, is both useful and easy to make. The materials are available at craft shops and home improvement centers. For each rack you will need a 2-foot length of wood about 1-inch square; 8 dowels (1/4-inch in diameter by 12 inches long); a small brass screw hook; sandpaper; wood stain; and a drill with a 1/4-inch bit.

Measure and mark the square stick 3 inches and 9 inches from each end. Number the sides lightly in order with a pencil, 1, 2, 3, 4. At the top 3-inch mark, drill straight through from side 1 to side 3. At the next mark drill from side 2 to side 4, then from side 1 to 3 and end with a hole from side 2 to 4. Sand around the holes.

Screw the brass hook into the top of the stick. Smooth the ends of the dowels with sandpaper and push them into the holes. The fit should be snug; if it is not, put a drop of wood glue in the hole, being careful to keep it off the rest of the wood. Stain the rack and allow it to dry thoroughly. If the surface is rough after staining, sand very lightly to smooth it.

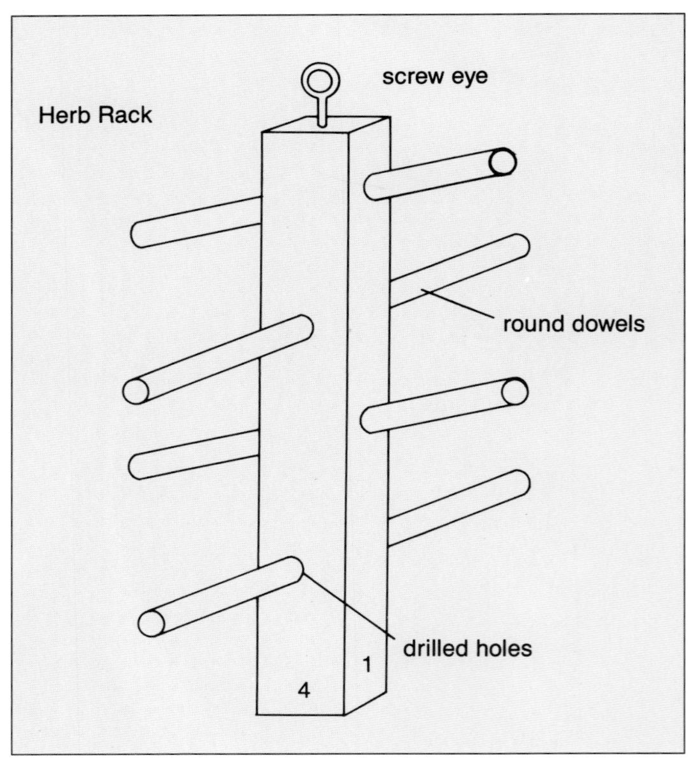

Candles

Unlike most other early lighting devices, the candle has never become obsolete. It has simply changed from being a necessity to being a warm accent and symbol of hospitality.

It is important that you use candle wax to make candles, not paraffin, which has a lower melting point. You will also need woven wicking. Both of these are available at craft supply stores.

You will need a container as deep as your candle will be long, such as a large juice can, and a deep kettle for water. Set the can of wax inside a kettle of boiling water and heat it to between 165°F and 170°F. Wax that is too cool will thicken and make dipping difficult, while wax that is too hot will melt off the previous layer. Once the wax is hot enough, you can remove the pan from the stove and work until the wax begins to cool.

Cut a wick twice the length of your candles, plus 3 inches. Tie the wick over a stick, looping it in two half-hitches so the wicks hang down about 2 inches apart. Dip both wicks into the wax, lift them out and let the excess wax drip back into the container until the wicks are cool enough to touch. Pull each wick straight. (You only need to pull after the initial dipping.) Continue dipping, letting the wax cool a little between dips, until the candles are the desired thickness. If you are making thin tapers, be sure they are sturdy enough to stand firmly.

Allow the finished candles to harden overnight before trimming their bases with a sharp knife. Leave them in pairs until you use them.

Cinnamon Swags and Bundles

Stick cinnamon is fragrant, flavorful and attractive. Bundles of cinnamon tied with bright red ribbons can scent and decorate your home, and you'll always have cinnamon sticks handy for seasoning hot drinks and jelly.

Tie the cinnamon bundles with gingham and calico ribbons. Make a bow and trim the ends at an angle. These make attractive holders for place cards at dinner parties and are nice additions to gift baskets of food.

Longer swags should be made of eight to ten sticks of uneven lengths. These may be hung on the wall or stood up in earthenware mugs.

Sachets

Little bundles of potpourri can be as plain or as fancy as your time, materials, imagination and energy dictate. At their simplest they are squares of fabric filled with spices and tied into bundles. At their fanciest, they are created in needlework techniques such as cross stitch, patchwork, appliqué or embroidery.

The variety of fabrics available today offers a number of possibilities for sachets that are easy to sew and require almost no decoration. Designs are printed in handy squares, some in patchwork patterns, others with sheep, barns or other country motifs. To make these into sachets, all you have to do is cut around the printed outlines and stitch them together, right sides facing, leaving a space for filling. Fill it with potpourri and sew the opening shut. A trim of matching eyelet can be added at the edge, or a matching bowstitched at one corner.

© Susanna Pashko/Envision

Wooden Sachets

Perhaps the easiest of all sachets to make, these are simply wooden balls or other shapes that have been permeated with fragrant essential oils—the same oils used in making potpourri. These are handy for refreshing the inside of shoes or boots, or for dropping into drawers, sewing baskets, purses or beach bags.

Craft suppliers have a variety of small wooden shapes, including spheres, acorns and thick, flat hearts. Place these shapes in a plastic bag and add a cotton ball which has been soaked in oil. Seal the bag and toss it so that each piece of wood is well coated. Leave the bag closed for at least a week, tossing it every day until the oil has thoroughly penetrated the wood. Fill a small jar with them, label it with suggested uses and give it as a gift.

Stenciled Baskets

Split baskets, the sturdy storage and picnic baskets made of thinly split wood cut into wide strips, are a mainstay of the country household. They are used for storage, for laundry, for gathering produce, for transporting pies and hot dishes, for picnics and for nearly anything else that needs a container.

They are also perfect stenciling surfaces. The broad wooden rim and the wide horizontal weaves provide flat surfaces just right for small stenciled designs. Flowers, hearts, strawberries, apples, watermelon and other simple designs work well on baskets. Avoid complicated patterns, since they are done against a busy background.

Flexible stencils are better on baskets than metal ones, since the surface is slightly curved. Use purchased stencils or cut your own by tracing any of these patterns onto mylar.™

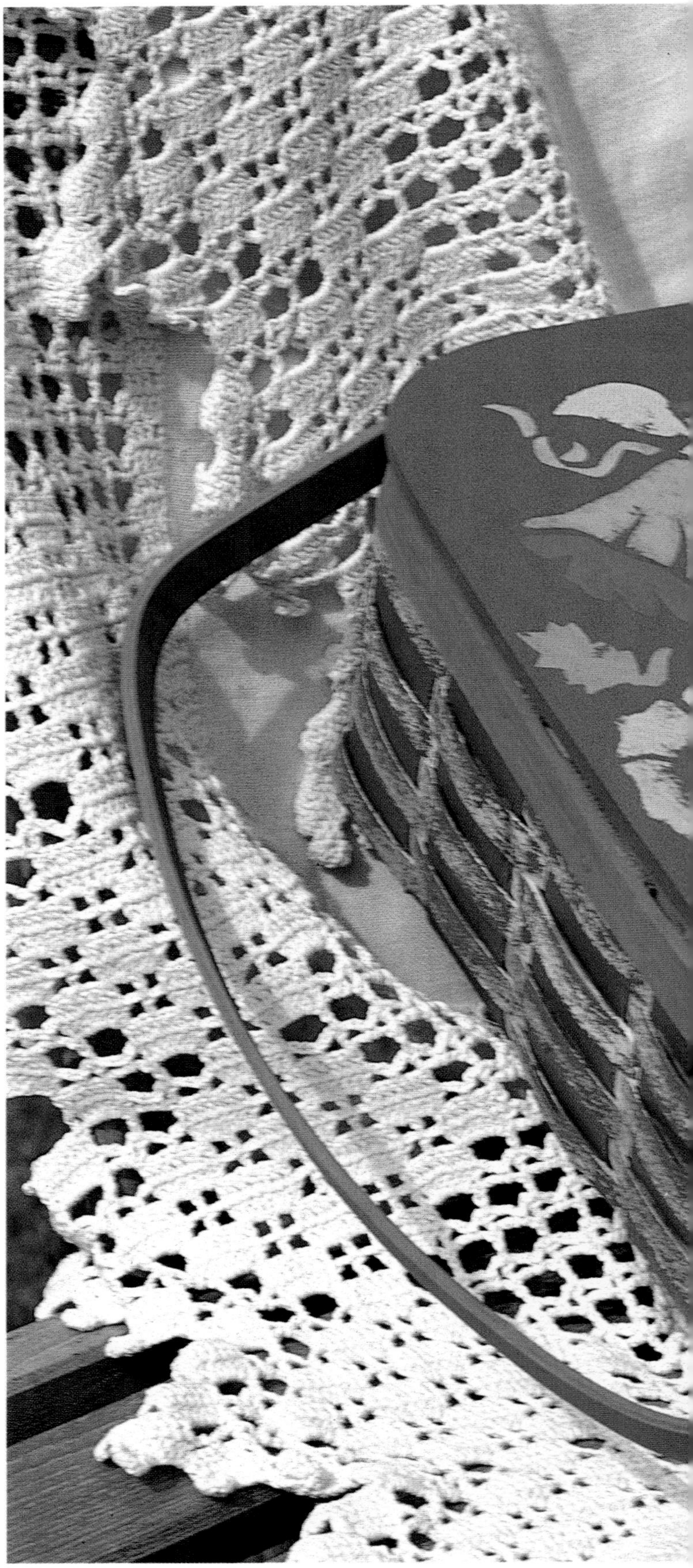

Stenciled Muslin Sachets

Unbleached muslin is a favorite with country decorators, especially those who enjoy stenciling. Little stenciled drawstring bags make generous sachets and cedar bags to hang in your closets. If you can't find these little ready-made bags in craft or potpourri shops, you can make your own by stitching 6-inch squares of muslin into bags, trimming the tops with pinking scissors and tying them shut with a ribbon or jute twine. Stencil these with simple designs and be sure to slip a piece of cardboard into the bag to keep the paint from soaking through to the other side. Stencil both sides, then fill and tie it.

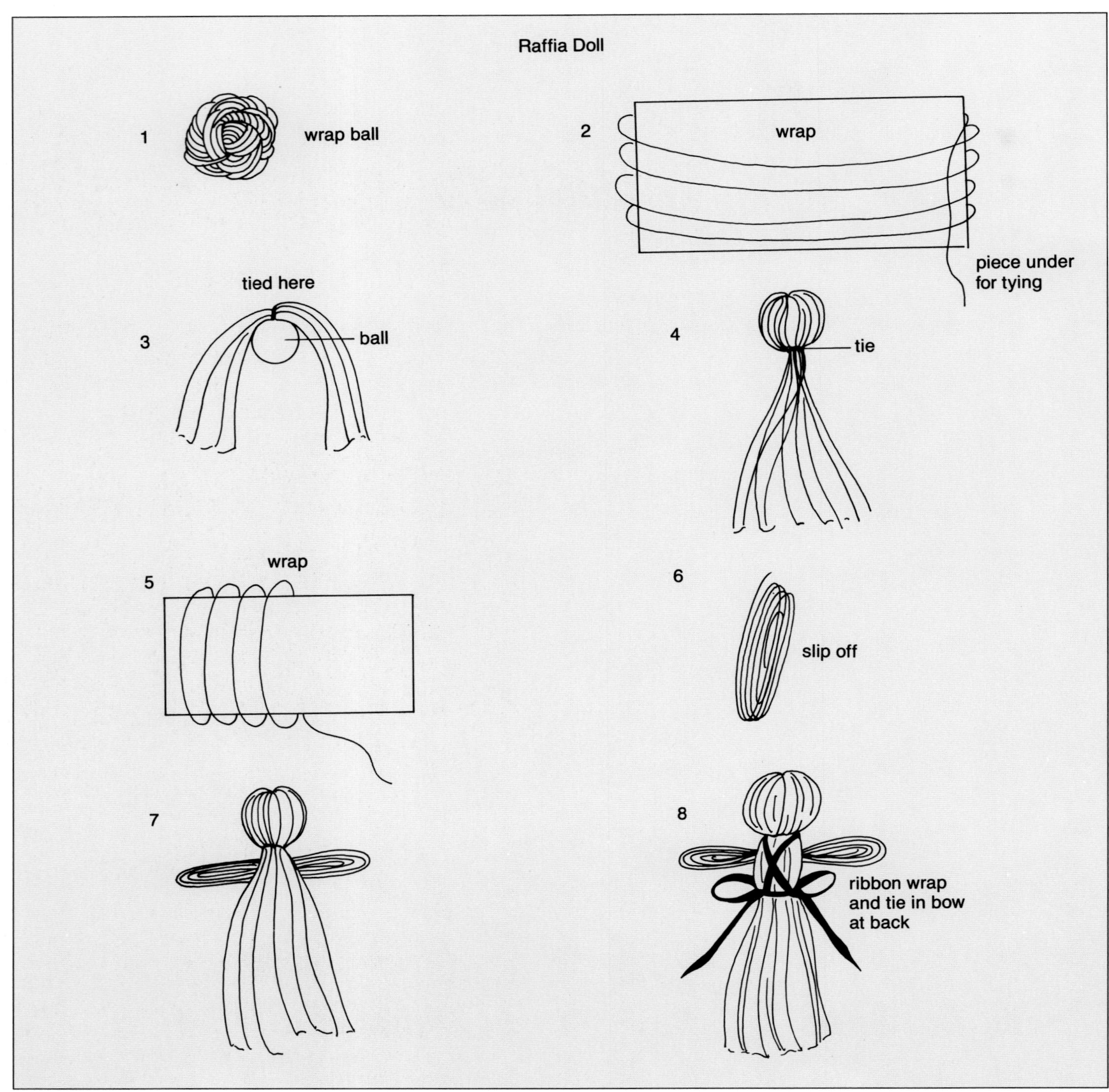

Raffia Dolls

Raffia is a versatile natural craft material that blends well with country surroundings. It is strong, pliable, soft and easy to work with. Unlike reed, cane and cornhusks, it does not have to be wet before it's worked with.

To make a raffia doll: 1) Wrap a length of raffia into a small ball. 2) Wrap about 12 rounds of raffia around a 6-inch strip of cardboard, running a strand underneath to hold it. Cut the other end. Pull both ends very tight and tie a knot. 3) Pull the raffia loops off the cardboard and place the wrapped ball right under the tie and spread the raffia to form a head. 4) Gather the raffia and tie it under the ball to make a neck. 5) Wind about 8 wraps of raffia around a 3½-inch width of cardboard. 6) Slip them off in one bunch without cutting them. 7) Separate the raffia from front to back just under the neck, and slide the bundle in to form arms. Tie just under the arms. 8) Wrap very narrow satin ribbon around the back of the neck and across the chest, and tie it at the back of the waist. Tie the raffia ends at the top of the head to make a loop for hanging.

Gifts From a Country Kitchen

Few gifts are as delightful as homemade food. A simple loaf of fruit bread, a jar of preserves or an entire basket of delicacies is a gift that compliments and pleases the recipient.

Although preserves, cookies and candy are among the most common gifts of homemade edibles, they are certainly not the only choices. For those who enjoy entertaining, a basket of interesting nibbles, such as patés, cheese spreads, crackers, bread sticks, pickled jalepeños and spiced nuts would be welcome.

For the good cook, a selection of ingredients, seasonings and condiments for the pantry might be the answer—try giving herb vinegar, homemade pasta, herb blends, mustard, hot-wings coating, a string of hot peppers or shallots.

© Robert Reck

Herb Fettuccini

$1\frac{1}{2}$ c. flour
1 egg
1 egg white
1 tbsp. olive oil
$\frac{1}{2}$ tsp. each, basil and oregano
1 tsp. salt
a few drops of water

Combine all the ingredients except the water in a large bowl and knead with fingers to form a dough. Add water to gather the crumbly pieces, and knead dough well until it is smooth and elastic. Wrap in waxed paper and allow to stand for 15 minutes. If you have a pasta machine, you can use it to roll the dough; otherwise, use a rolling pin. Working with one-quarter of the dough at a time, roll it as thin as possible. Cut into $\frac{1}{4}$-inch-wide strips and hang these over a suspended dowel or rack until dry. To present, simply package in a plastic bag tied with a colorful ribbon.

Makes $\frac{1}{2}$ pound of dry pasta.

Port Wine Cheddar Spread

$\frac{1}{2}$ lb. Cheddar cheese
$\frac{1}{4}$ c. Port wine

Shred cheese and place in a blender with port. Blend until smooth, adding more wine if necessary to make a smooth spread. This is attractive presented in a crock or a pottery cup, which can be stored in the refrigerator and brought right to the cocktail table for serving.

C · H · A · P · T · E · R

3

Preserving the Harvest

Putting up the bounty of a summer's harvest is a time-honored country tradition. Farm families everywhere take pride in the neat rows of crisp pickles, sparkling jellies and bright vegetables and fruits that line their pantry shelves.

Although freezing has largely replaced canning of most vegetables and fruit—it is both faster and easier, and it preserves the texture and quality better—there is no substitute for homemade pickles, relishes, conserves, butters and jams. None of them is difficult to make, and the results are well worth the effort.

Despite the mystique that surrounds perfect pickles and jellies, there are very few tricks to fine preserving. Be sure that all your utensils are clean and sterile. Jars should be boiled for ten minutes just before they are filled. Follow the manufacturer's directions for preparing the lids. Sealed jars should be be processed for fifteen minutes in boiling water to assure a perfect seal. Although most older recipes do not call for this, research has determined that it is necessary. You should process all recipes, even jellies. Paraffin seals are not safe. All products should be put in jars with rubber-lined lids.

The only other general rule is to use fresh, perfect produce. Jam is not the place for squishy fruit or bruised berries, and pickles made from last week's cucumbers will be soggy, not crisp.

Preserving vegetables and fruits used to be the only way to have fresh-tasting food all winter; today it's as much a labor of love as of necessity. This woman has the perfect country kitchen, with plenty of pots and pans and lots of room. But you don't need a huge kitchen to can and pickle foods. You can even do it in your city home.

© Michael Keller/FPG International

The process of pickling is quite simple. Vegetables are cut or sliced, sometimes soaked in ice or saltwater, and cooked briefly in a brine made of vinegar, sugar and spices. The vegetables are removed, packed into hot jars and the brine poured over them. The sealed jars are then processed in boiling water to insure an airtight seal. Relishes follow the same procedure but use finely cut or ground vegetables.

For jellies, fruit is combined with sugar, then boiled until drops of the hot mixture slide from a large spoon in a sheet instead of separate drops. Preserves are made with whole or large-cut fruit, jams with crushed fruit.

Jelly is made by cooking the clear juice strained from cooked fruit and boiling it to the jelly stage as above. Some fruits that lack pectin, such as peaches, can be made into jelly by adding pectin-rich fruit such as apples, or using a commercial pectin. Each of these is different, so always follow the recipe.

Conserves and chutney are similar to jams, but have added ingredients such as nuts and raisins. Chutney is made with vinegar, requires less sugar, and does not jell.

© R. Embery/FPG International

APPLE BUTTER

Simply stated, butters are fruit purées cooked slowly with a minimum of sugar until they are a thick, but spreadable, consistency.

5 lbs. apples, quartered
2 c. apple cider
sugar
cinnamon
cloves
allspice

Wash and quarter apples and simmer over low heat in one inch of water until the apples soften. Mash them down as they cook.

Put them through the food mill and measure the pulp. Meanwhile boil the apple cider down to less than 1 cup. Add the cider to the pulp along with half as much sugar as there is pulp. Add cinnamon, cloves and allspice to taste—about 1/2 teaspoon combined for each 2 cups of pulp. Bring to a boil and cook uncovered over very low heat until most of the liquid has evaporated. Stir it frequently since it sticks very easily.

When there is very little juice left, transfer to a flat glass or pottery baking dish and bake uncovered in a 250°F oven, stirring every 15 minutes. In about 3 or 4 hours, the apple butter will be a rich brown color, stand up on a spoon, and smell divine. Spoon it into hot sterile jars, seal and process for 15 minutes.

PEACH BUTTER

fresh peaches, sliced
brown sugar
lemon juice
ground ginger

Peach butter is also delicious. Peel and stone peaches and simmer them in just enough water to keep them from sticking, mashing them as they cook. When they are soft, purée them and measure the pulp. Add half as much brown sugar as there is pulp, and the juice of one lemon and 1/2 teaspoon of ground ginger for every 2 cups of pulp.

Cook on the stove over very low heat until the mixture is thick and dark. Stir it often. When it is ready, seal in sterile jars and process for 15 minutes.

GRAPE CONSERVE

3 lbs. ripe Concord grapes
1 lb. raisins
peel of one orange, chopped
juice of one orange
2 1/2 c. sugar
1/2 tsp. cinnamon
1 sprig fresh thyme
1 c. chopped pecans

Pop the skins from the grapes; do not discard. In a saucepan over low heat, cook the grapes briefly and put through a food mill to remove the seeds. Grind the skins with the raisins. Combine all the ingredients except the nuts and cook slowly until thick (about 1 1/2 hours). Add the pecans and cook 5 minutes longer. Seal in hot jars and process for 15 minutes.

Mickey's Bread and Butter Pickles

2 qts. thinly sliced cucumbers
2 medium onions, sliced
1 garlic clove, sliced thin
1/4 c. salt
1 1/2 c. sugar
1 1/4 c. cider vinegar
1 tbsp. mustard seed
1/2 tsp. turmeric
1/2 tsp. celery seed

Combine cucumber, onion, garlic and salt and cover with crushed ice. Stir occasionally for 3 hours. Drain and rinse well. Combine the remaining ingredients with the cucumbers in a pan, bring to a boil for 5 minutes. Add water if there is not enough juice to cover the vegetables. Pour pickles into hot, sterilized jars, seal and process for 15 minutes in boiling water.

Makes approximately 2 quarts of pickles.

Pickled Jalapeños

jalapeño peppers
cider vinegar

Wash the peppers well and pierce in several places with the tip of a knife. Pack peppers as snugly as possible in hot jars. Bring vinegar to a boil and fill the jars. Seal and process for 15 minutes. To use peppers in recipes calling for fresh jalapeños, simply rinse them in cold water first.

Piccalilli

6 green tomatoes
4 green peppers
2 sweet red peppers
1 hot pepper
5 onions
1/4 c. salt
2 1/2 c. brown sugar
1 3/4 c. cider vinegar
1 tbsp. mustard seed
1 tbsp. whole allspice
1 tsp. celery seed
1 tsp. whole cloves

Slice all the vegetables very thin, toss with salt and let sit overnight. Rinse in cold water and drain well. Combine in a large pot with the remaining ingredients, bring to a boil, and simmer for 15 minutes. Seal in hot jars and process for 15 minutes.

Crab Apple Jelly

Cut several pounds of crab apples in half, barely cover them in water and simmer. When crab apples are soft, mash and continue cooking for 5 minutes. Pour into a jelly bag and allow to drip overnight. Do not squeeze. Measure juice and combine with an equal amount of sugar. Boil to the jelly point, which will probably take only a few minutes, unless the apples have been stored for a long time. Skim froth from top and ladle into hot jars. Seal and process for 15 minutes.

© James Church/FPG International

Peach Chutney

5 lbs. peaches
1/2 lb. raisins
1/2 lb. dates, chopped
1 lemon, thinly sliced
2 c. vinegar
3 c. sugar
1/2 c. fresh lemon or lime juice
1/2 c. candied ginger, chopped

Peel and chop the peaches. Combine all the ingredients and cook until thick, stirring often. Seal in hot jars and process for 15 minutes.

© Myrleen Ferguson/PhotoEdit

© F. Stein/FPG International

Dill Pickles

To make crisp dill pickles, use whole small cucumbers, freshly picked.

fresh, small whole cucumbers
3/4 c. pickling salt
2 1/2 qts. water
1/2 c. vinegar
dill heads
a few garlic cloves (optional)
hot pepper (optional)

Make a brine with the pickling salt, water and vinegar. Heat to dissolve the salt and let cool before using. Alternate layers of cucumbers in a crock with heads of dill. Add garlic cloves and a hot pepper to add character to the pickles, if desired.

Pour the brine over the vegetables and cover with a cloth, plate and weight. Remove the scum daily as with the sauerkraut. In 2 weeks, pack the vegetables in hot sterile jars. Heat to boiling 4 quarts of water, 1 quart vinegar and 1/2 cup pickling salt. Pour it over the vegetables and seal jars. Process for 15 minutes.

Sauerkraut

Homemade sauerkraut has no equal in either can or jar or at the deli counter. This recipe is for a one-gallon container.

5 lbs. cabbage
3 tbsp. kosher or pickling salt (NOT iodized table salt)

Shred the cabbage. Alternate layers of cabbage in your container with a sprinkling of salt, tapping each layer with a wooden masher. The top layer should be salt. This will not seem like enough salt, but it will give you a 2 1/2 percent solution, just the right strength for fermentation.

Boil an old dish towel in water for 5 minutes and cover the crock with it. Weight this down with a plate close to the diameter of the inside of the crock and weight that with a canning jar filled with water. You should have enough brine by the next day to cover the cabbage. If not, add sufficient brine in the proportions of 1 1/2 teaspoons of salt to 1 cup of water.

In 2 or 3 days, white scum will form on the top. Skim this off, and replace the cloth with a newly boiled one. Wash the plate and replace it. Repeat this (a 5-minute job) each day until the bubbles stop rising. Then your sauerkraut is done. This takes about 2 weeks.

Winning Blue Ribbons at the Fair

Crystal shimmering jellies and bright, translucent pickles are a trademark of country fairs, as are the bright blue ribbons that hang from the jars. Some of those blue ribbons could be hanging from your homemade preserves. There are no secrets, but there are a few things you should know.

At some fairs, jars are not opened; a good preserved product can proclaim its quality right through the glass. And a good judge can tell just how good your strawberry preserves are without tasting them.

Judges recognize pickles with too much vinegar (they shrivel), or fruit that has been allowed to sit too long between picking and packing. So follow the rules of good preparation and preserving first, then take a little extra care with each jar.

Pack all the jars evenly—all pickles the same size, pickle slices set against the edge of the jar in even rows, and so on. Jellies need to be perfectly clear, so let the juice strain in the refrigerator overnight and pour off the top juice, leaving any sediment on the bottom.

Store jars without their metal rings until you are ready to pack for the fair. A day or two before, bring jars from the cellar and let them adjust to room temperature. Quickly dip each jar into barely simmering water to which a little vinegar has been added and let drain on a towel. This makes the jars shine. Relabel each jar according to fair rules.

After the judging, look at the other blue-ribbon jars for ideas on how you can improve—chances are good that other hopeful entrants will be looking at some of your blue-ribbon jars for the same reason.

Kerr
SELF SEALING
MASON

© Ken Ross/Viesti Associates, Inc.

Onion Braids, Pepper Strings, Dried Apples

In a Mediterranean country kitchen, long braids of onions, shallots and garlic and strings of bright red peppers decorate the walls with handy ingredients for the cook. Strings of drying apples are a common sight in a Pennsylvania Dutch farmhouse, while ears of popcorn or grinding corn drying on an iron "drying tree" may be seen from New England to the Southwest.

The purpose in hanging onions and garlic is not to dry it, but to store it in an airy place where it will keep well, but be handy for use. Hot peppers, corn and apples are left hanging until they are completely dry, when they may be stored in containers.

You can braid the long stalks of onions, garlic and shallots into strings. When the tops are dry but not brittle, tie three of them together and begin braiding. As soon as the braid is long enough, add an onion, shallot or garlic bulb to the braid, and continue adding as you braid to make a tight column of bulbs. When the string is long enough, tie the braid and cut off the remaining stalk ends.

Hot peppers such as the red Italian variety can be strung on long threads to dry, or you can braid jute cord tightly, slipping pepper strings into the braid as you work.

Popcorn, seed corn and grinding corn can also be braided by their husks or tied into bundles for drying. Corn looks especially good on "drying trees," which hold the ears separately.

To dry apples, peel, core and slice firm apples into thin rings and drop them into a bowl of water with lemon juice squeezed into it. Don't leave them there more than ten minutes. Remove and pat them dry. Thread these on a long string and hang them in a clean, airy place, separating the rings. When they become leathery, they are dry enough, and should then be stored in a tightly closed jar.

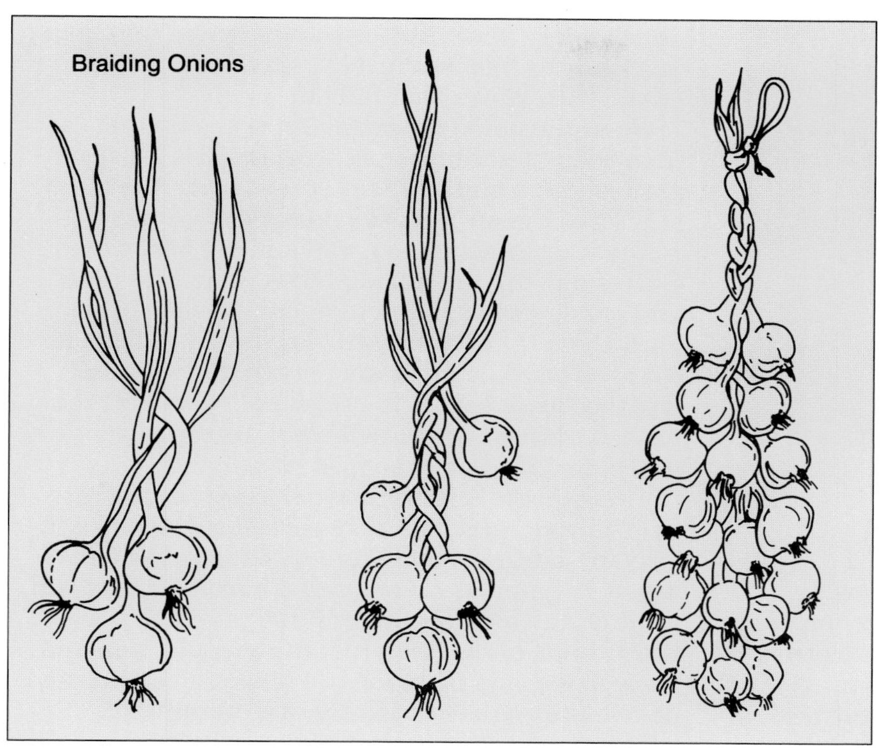

© Jerry Howard/Positive Images

© Rogers Associates

Drying and Preserving Herbs

Most herbs (See, A Bouquet of Herbs to Grow, pages 98–99) can be dried for use in the kitchen. For the best flavor, harvest before the plant blooms, cutting the entire stem. Harvest in the morning, after the dew has dried, but before the heat of the midday sun. Tie herbs in bunches and hang in a shaded, airy place. To protect the leaves from dust, suspend the bunches inside paper bags, which catch dried leaves that fall off.

When the herbs are crisp and dry, strip them from their stems and store in glass jars. This is a good job for a blustery winter day, when the herbs will scent the air with the promise of spring.

A few herbs do not dry well and are best frozen. Chives and dill are among these, as well as basil and parsley which often turn brown when dried. Pack them tightly in plastic bags with as little air space as possible, to preserve both the color and flavor of these herbs. To use, simply shave off the needed amount which will thaw instantly into green, fresh-looking chopped herbs.

Vinegars are another way of preserving fresh herb flavors, which quickly permeate the vinegar. Use any herb you would use in salads—basil, marjoram, oregano, tarragon, salad burnet, chives, dill, mint or any blend of these. Fill a jar about one-third full of herbs, then fill with vinegar, seal and store in a shady place for two weeks. The vinegar is delicious on salads (or, in the case of mint, on grilled or roasted lamb).

© Jerry Howard/Positive Images

© Jerry Howard/Positive Images

© Envision

C · H · A · P · T · E · R

4

The Country Garden

It is difficult to pinpoint just what separates a country garden from all others. It isn't its size or its location; it isn't how well it is tended or what kinds of plants it contains. A country garden can flourish in a very small space, barely contained by a picket fence from spilling out onto a busy sidewalk.

There is, however, a special feeling to a country garden, a freedom, an exuberance—whether it grows old roses and gillyflowers or cactus and ornamental grasses. A country garden isn't fussy or pretentious, or clipped like a poodle or held into elaborately shaped little beds. Yet some of the world's loveliest country gardens sit in sculptured terraces among the manicured lawns of English stately homes.

Simply stated, a country garden looks as if it grew naturally, and wasn't planted by a gardener. It fits in with its surroundings—the home, the terrain, the scenery—and it is not only a delight to look at, it is intended to be used. It can be strolled in, cut and brought indoors for a quick bouquet, sniffed on the evening breeze or clipped to garnish a luncheon sandwich.

Whatever garden layout you choose, it can be a part of your landscaping plan. Borders are a favorite in landscape design—they're easy to reach and keep up, change with the seasons and can hide a less-than-lovely foundation or wall.

Country gardens have a freedom that comes from mixing a variety of colors and styles that look natural together. Country gardens don't look like they're fussed and fawned over—though some certainly are. They have a fresh exuberance about them that is very appealing.

© Nancy Hill

© Lynn Karlin

© William Seitz

Flower borders can accent a building or diminish it, outline a vegetable garden or terrace or border a walk or driveway.

They are beautiful beside a stone wall, or as a graceful crown for a retaining wall. In front of a fence, wall, building or other backdrop, plant tall flowers nearest the wall and short ones in front. When selecting border plants, avoid spreading or very bushy species. Tall delphinium, foxglove, hollyhocks, shasta daisies, achillea and phlox are best as background plants, while pinks, zinnias, cornflowers and calendula fill the center. Nasturtiums, French marigolds, sweet William and silver mound artemisia often line bed fronts in compact mounds that hide the stems of plants behind them.

Freestanding borders, along a drive or walkway, are planted like an "A"—tall flowers along the center, shorter flowers tapering toward the edges. Freestanding flower beds present different opportunities as well as challenges. They are the place for large, bushy plants such as baptisia and baby's breath, as well as spreading clumps of daylilies. Columbine and bluebells can be interspersed with smaller plants and bordered with low-growing clumps of more fragile flowers such as coral bells, which would be lost in most borders.

While balancing the size and growing habits of the flowers, one also needs to remember the seasonal nature of perennials. Each has its own cycle and its own timetable. The first spring blossoms are bulbs—crocus, which can grow right

through your lawn and be mowed over later, tulips, whose foliage dies in time to be covered with annual beds, and daffodils, whose clumps of narrow leaves can be braided and tucked under the foliage of later perennials.

Along with the bulbs come the dainty violets and pasqueflowers. These are followed by irises, thrift, primrose, mallows and yellow globe flowers, then poppies, delphinium, foxglove and achillea. Careful gardeners will also want to include some that continue to bloom through the fall—coreopsis, golden marguerite, heliopsis, coral bells and basket flowers.

While some gardeners cut from the array in their flower beds, others prefer to plant cutting flowers in rows in the vegetable garden or in a special cutting garden where a bouquet for the dining room table will not leave the front border bare. A cutting garden is also the best place for some drying flowers, such as annual statice and strawflowers, which can be ungainly, rangy plants.

Shady patches at the edge of the woods are just right for a garden of woodland wildflowers—jack-in-the-pulpit, ladies' slippers, trillium and hepaticas flourish here as do columbine, periwinkles and some spring bulbs.

Wherever you plant your flowers, the garden should work with the land, not against it. Choose cascading, creeping phlox for the tops of walls and steep embankments, clumps of violets to peek from between rocks in a wall, and tall dramatic flowers where you need character.

© Nancy Hill

© Nancy Hill

A Garden Off the Kitchen

Traditionally, the kitchen garden was only a few steps from the kitchen door. Herbs, salad vegetables such as greens and radishes, a pepper plant, green onions and a tomato plant grew here—enough for the few vegetables needed quickly for the preparation of a meal. The corn, beans, pumpkins, squash, beets, potatoes and other staple crops were in the "big garden."

Modern gardeners find the idea of a small garden near the kitchen door appealing, since it often holds all of the herbs and vegetables needed. It can be kept small and tidy, and is handy and easy to tend. Because of its size, it is suitable for raised beds, which bring the plants into easy reach. For those who wish to grow only a few fresh salad vegetables and herbs, the kitchen garden is the perfect answer.

© Nancy Hill

© Anita Sabarese

© Nancy Hill

Gardens For Patios, Balconies And Tiny Spaces

Container gardening has become so popular with people who want to enjoy a country garden in the city, that seed houses have developed strains especially for container growing. These gardens have many advantages: no hoeing, little weeding, no strenuous labor. And they can be moved to a new home quite easily. However, like house pets, container gardens need more attention than their free-roaming counterparts. Without deep soil for water and nutrients, they must be fed and watered frequently.

Choosing containers can be as much fun as choosing plants. Clay pots, wine barrels, wooden planter boxes and window boxes are only a few of the items that make good planters. Porous materials such as terra cotta and untreated wood allow air and water to circulate, but also dry out the soil easily, so plants in these containers will require more water. In hot, dry climates, non porous materials such as glazed ceramic, plastic and lined wood might be better choices.

© FPG International

All containers must have drainage holes or several inches of coarse gravel in the bottom of the pot. Setting pots on platforms helps insure air circulation and protects patio surfaces from staining. Bases with wheels are easier to move if you need to follow the sun from one spot to another.

Be sure to use sterile potting soil (never garden dirt), for a perfect moisture-retaining texture which is designed for proper drainage. Moisten the soil lightly before planting, but don't soak it. Water daily as needed—test soil first with fingers. Plants may need even more frequent watering in hot or windy weather. Plants take in both food and water through the roots, so a thirsty plant is also a hungry plant. Water until the excess runs freely out the drainage holes.

Choose pot locations according to the needs of each plant—full sun for peppers and tomatoes, partial shade for herbs and salad greens. Look for bush tomatoes and cucumbers, miniature and compact lettuces and greens, and small herb varieties Shepherd's Garden Seeds (see Appendix) offers many varieties especially developed for small patio gardens.

The Country Herb Garden

While an herb garden won't exactly grow by itself, herbs are among the least demanding plants. Once established they withstand drought, indifferent soil, blazing sun and inattention. They thrive with tender loving care, but also will survive without it.

Attractive in the garden, tasty on the table and fragrant decorations for your kitchen, they are among the most rewarding and useful plants. Grow them in borders, flower beds and vegetable gardens, in clumps by the kitchen door or in separate little plots all their own. With a few exceptions, most culinary herbs remain tidy and attractive in the garden.

Even in a country setting, herbs lend themselves to little garden plots where varieties can be kept separate. Herb beds are often planted in shapes—square with diagonal crossed paths, round with radiating wedge-shaped beds.

Although you can plant an herb garden from seed, it takes care and patience, with little reward in the first year or so. To give your herb garden a head start, begin with a few sturdy nursery plants that will provide attractive growth and a harvest the first season.

Once plants are growing well you can begin using them. The best way to cut most herbs for kitchen use is to take the tips of several branches instead of one whole piece. This encourages them to grow thicker and bushier. Plants that grow in clumps right from the root, such as chives or salad burnet, should be clipped close to the ground. Never cut chives across the top as though you were trimming a hedge; always take entire leaves from the base.

© Envision

© Jerry Howard/Positive Images

© Anita Sabarese

© Susanna Pashko/Envision

Reading The Seed Catalog

The first thing to remember is that seed catalogs, except for the few geared especially to regional gardeners, are designed to be used by gardeners from Canada to Texas. Look for crops that will perform well in your climate. Varieties labeled *drought resistant* are right for the Southwest, *slow to bolt* for the South, and *early producing* for the North. Experimental gardens all over the continent are busy breeding vegetables for all climates, so be sure you choose the seeds for yours.

Some seed catalogs cater to the small gardener who needs only a few plants of each variety. The Cook's Garden (see Appendix) is one of these, offering a single packet with a fine selection of different salad greens. These are divided by season, so you can have six or eight early spring greens, as many mid-summer, and another selection for fall from just three packets.

Seed catalogs are often packed with information, not only on the varieties, but on gardening as well. Johnny's Selected Seeds (see Appendix) publishes such a catalog; you can learn a lot about gardening just from reading these.

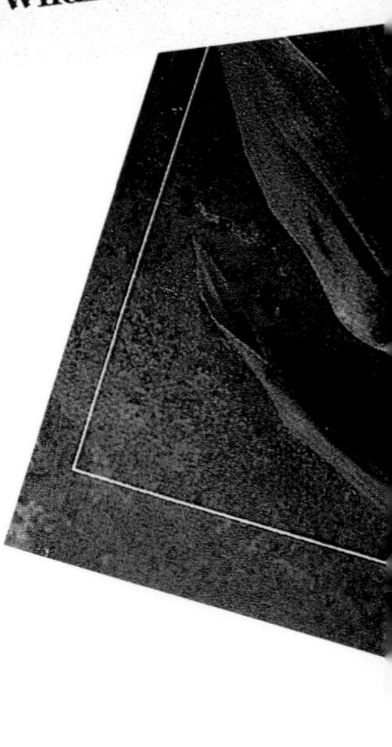

For copies of the catalogs pictured here, write:

The Vermont Wildflower Farm
Route 7
Charlotte, VT 05445

W. Atlee Burpee Seed Co.
300 Park Ave.
Warminster, PA 18974

Wayside Gardens
Hodges, SC 29695

Mellinger's
2310 West South Range Rd.
North Lima, OH 44452

Growing Perennials

Since perennials grow year after year, they tend to develop more slowly than annuals, rarely flowering the first year. They usually are started from plants, often taken from well-developed clumps by root division. It is important to know how quickly plants spread so you will know how much room to leave between them. Smaller plants set between newly planted larger ones can be moved to new locations as the larger plants spread.

Perennials usually have a shorter bloom period than annuals, so choose a few that flower at different times to keep your garden in continual bloom. Don't forget to include flowering shrubs such as forsythia and azalea in your plan.

Soil should be free of weeds and grass, and dug deeply since perennial growth depends on a sturdy root system. If soil is sandy, be sure to add some organic material to help it retain moisture. If you are using plants from a greenhouse, harden off the tender stems and leaves by putting them outdoors in their pots for a few hours each day for about a week before planting. Avoid hot, sunny middays for transplanting and keep plants well watered for the first week or so.

© Patrick Walmsley/Envision

Growing Annuals

If you have sunny windows and a little patience, you may have fun growing at least some annuals from seed. Garden supply stores carry plastic trays with lids and bases, so you can create a windowsill greenhouse late in the winter.

When seeds sprout, pinch out all but the strongest plant in each pot. By the time the weather is settled enough for planting, you may have to move some of them to larger pots. Favorites to start from seed are marigolds, zinnias, calendula, snapdragon and cornflowers.

Some annuals grow better if they are seeded in the ground. Nasturtium, for example, will produce abundant, lush foliage but very few flowers if it is transplanted. The neat, colorful border you anticipated may well become a green jungle, choking out the taller flowers behind.

Since annuals are quick-growing, they usually bloom for a long period if the fading flowers are kept picked off. If the flowers dry on the plant and form seeds, the plant finishes its reproductive cycle and will not continue to bloom. So pick bouquets often, or at least remember to snap off faded blossoms.

© Anita Sabarese

A Bouquet of Herbs to Grow

BASIL *(Ocimum basilicum):* An annual, basil often grows to twenty-four inches. It is most commonly used in salads, with tomatoes and in pesto. If you plan to use it for the latter, plant several, since one batch of pesto can use an entire plant. Pinch off the flowering stems to encourage better leaf growth. Be sure to protect basil at the first hint of frost, since it is the most sensitive of all garden plants.

© Anita Sabarese

BEEBALM *(Monarda didyma):* This is a tall, stately perennial with red, pink or white blossoms; the leaves give Earl Gray tea its distinctive flavor. Use its fragrant, buttonlike dried heads in arrangements and wreaths. Allow it room in the garden to spread.

CHIVES *(Allium schoenoprasum):* This perennial spreads quickly, forming attractive clumps. Its delicate onion flavor complements salads, eggs, potatoes and cottage cheese. The pink blossoms, too, are good in salads or scrambled eggs. Chives grow 12 to 18 inches tall and make an attractive border behind other plants. A variety is the garlic chive, which has flat leaves, white flowers and a distinctive garlic flavor that is pleasant in salads.

DILL *(Anethum graveolens):* An annual, three to four feet tall. Plant dill in clumps so its long stems can support each other. Dill is best grown from seed, since its roots are so short and fragile that they often don't survive transplanting. Rake an area 1- to 3-feet square and scatter seeds generously. Rake again or sprinkle with soil and keep well watered until seedlings are strong. Dill leaves are good with fish or new potatoes.

MARJORAM *(Origanum majorana):* This perennial is a favorite seasoning in meats, salads, and in Italian and Greek dishes. Since there are several varieties, not all of them flavorful, ask if you can taste a leaf. If it doesn't have a clear flavor, it is not a culinary variety. Don't blame the nursery, however, since the varieties don't always run true and the labeling on seeds is often unclear. The nonculinary variety has lovely magenta flowers which dry very well for everlasting arrangements.

MINT *(Mentha):* A perennial, often 2 to 3 feet tall, mint spreads so quickly that it can easily take over a small garden, or even a lawn. Plant it in a large metal tub or bucket sunk right to its rim in the garden. Or, better yet, plant it at the edge of a field where it won't matter if it does spread. Use in cold drinks, in salads or for making jelly.

PARSLEY *(Petroselinum crispum):* A biennial, the two varieties of parsley, curly and Italian (which has a better flavor and texture), grow about 12 inches high. Plants will come back a second year and go quickly to seed, after which leaves are small and tough, so begin with new plants each spring. This herb is used as a garnish and to counter the aftertaste of garlic.

Herbs are attractive and useful plants to grow. These are (moving clockwise from top left) beebalm; dried marjoram flowers; thyme in bloom; and salad burnet.

SAGE *(Salvia):* This perennial can grow to a small shrub in a few years, so be sure to leave it plenty of room. Use it to flavor chicken and veal and in sausage. Trim it fairly close to the stem when cutting it in the fall, since it will die back anyway; close cutting makes it bushier the following year.

SALAD BURNET *(Poterium sanguisorba):* A perennial used raw in salads for its distinct cucumber flavor, it grows up to 12 inches tall in a neat mound which remains green until snow covers it.

TARRAGON *(Artemisia dracunculus):* A perennial, tarragon grows to 30 inches tall in good soil. French tarragon is better than the Russian variety, which has no flavor and grows rangy and tall, eventually over the entire garden. Use tarragon with fish or chicken.

THYME *(Thymus):* A perennial with many varieties, of which the so-called French or English are the best for general use. All are tidy, low-growing plants whose clumps expand outward each year. Use in soups and stews or with lamb, chicken or pork.

A Gallery of Flowers

BABY'S BREATH *(Gyposphila):* A perennial, baby's breath blooms in white, and occasionally pink. Its tiny flowers bloom at each tip of a finely branched stem. It retains its cloudlike look when dried. Used extensively as a filler in floral arrangements, it is also a favorite for wreaths. Pick the entire branch when most of the flowers are in bloom. Allow plenty of space in your garden for this plant, because although it does not spread, it is very bushy—like a white cloud in the garden.

BEARDED IRIS *(Iris germanica):* Perennials grown from rhizomes, these should remain partially visible above the soil when planted. The stately iris blooms in all shades from white to deep purple, including mauve and yellow. The blooming period may last for as long as four weeks in early summer.

CALENDULA *(Calendula):* Annuals easily grown from seed, you can start them indoors or sow them directly in the garden. They thrive in full sun and cool climates, growing between 12 and 18 inches tall. They are a favorite for potpourri, since they maintain their bright yellow and orange colors when dried.

CROCUS *(Crocus):* A perennial grown from bulbs planted in the fall, these often bloom before the last snowfall early in the spring. Colors include white, purple and yellow. Plant these cheerful flowers throughout your country lawn and mow over the foliage later in the spring.

This gallery of flowers includes (from left to right) delphinium; oriental poppy; a rose; and yucca.

DAYLILY *(Hemerocallis):* A perennial, this flower grows easily in sun or partial shade and reaches a height of about three feet. A very hardy plant, it spreads quickly and can be found beside old cellar holes where it has flourished without care for decades. Colors vary from yellow through orange.

DELPHINIUM *(Delphinium):* A perennial of blue and purple shades, it grows from three to five feet tall . Extend its short blooming season in early summer by picking individual blossoms as they begin to fade. If none of the blossoms is allowed to seed, delphinum will usually bloom again in the fall.

FEVERFEW *(Pyrethrum):* Perennials of the chrysanthemum family, these will bloom the first year if seeds are started early. Clusters of small daisylike flowers on sturdy 12- to 18-inch stems dry well—perfect for everlasting arrangements.

FORGET-ME-NOT *(Myosotis):* One of the earlier-blooming flowers, this annual will often self-sow in subsequent years. Forget-me-nots will grow in sun or shade, and prefer cool weather. They are very neat in the garden, where they are a favorite edging plant. In warmer climates, sow seeds directly in the garden in the fall.

© Anita Sabarese

© Nancy Hill

© Anita Sabarese

GLOBE FLOWER *(Trollius):* This perennial grows in tidy clumps covered with bright yellow blooms. A plant with an old-fashioned look, it blossoms early in the summer, long before most other yellow flowers. Its clumps may grow two feet tall, preferring rich, moist soil and thriving even in light shade.

MARIGOLDS *(Tagetes):* Easily grown from seed or purchased plants, this annual's compact mounds are usually about 12 inches tall; colors range from yellows to golden russets. They thrive in full sun, and do not require rich soil.

NASTURTIUM *(Tropaeolum):* An annual grown from seed planted directly in the garden, the flowers range from pale yellow to deep red, and they bloom best in full sun with sparse watering. They grow especially well in seaside gardens, and in window boxes where they trail nicely. Dwarf varieties usually grow in 12-inch mounds.

ORIENTAL POPPY *(Papaver):* A perennial of tall growth and little foliage, oriental poppies are one of the showiest, most dramatic and short-lived of all garden flowers. A blossom may last only a day or two, so plant in groups for a longer color season. Difficult to transplant once established, it is best to buy young plants from a nursery where they have been grown in pots.

PASQUEFLOWER *(Anemone):* A perennial, among the earliest to blossom in the spring, these low-growing lavender flowers thrive along rock walls where they get good drainage.

PINKS *(Dianthus):* Annual and perennial varieties related to carnations, pinks grow between twelve and eighteen inches tall. They have pale green foliage and bloom in shades of pink, white and rose. Even the perennial varieties will flower all summer long if you keep the spent flowers picked.

ROSE *(Rosa):* June-blooming varieties include many of the fragrant old roses, some of which are bush growing and others of which climb. While hybrid roses are favored for more formal settings, these old varieties are perfect for country gardens where they will wander over stone walls and fences. Several varieties produce rose hips, which dry well for tea as well as for use in arrangements or wreaths.

SIBERIAN IRIS *(Iris sibirica):* A perennial, this iris grows in round clumps of tall, graceful leaves. Its bright purple blossoms last well and bloom in mid-summer, after bearded irises have faded. About three feet tall, these clumps are best for beds, not for borders.

VIOLET *(Viola):* Perennials that spread by self-sowing, clumps of violets bloom in white and purple at the same time as daffodils. These create a very attractive combination, especially when they are planted along a rock wall.

YARROW *(Achillea):* A perennial in bright yellow, red and deep pink, it grows about three feet tall. Remarkably, yarrow thrives in poor soil. Large, flat clusters will bloom for several weeks in summer if the heads are kept picked. It is a favorite for everlasting arrangements if picked and dried just before it reaches full bloom. Clumps increase to create a showy display in a very few years.

YUCCA *(Yucca):* A perennial, yucca thrives in hot, dry climates, but will also grow in northern climates in full sun. Its showy clump of white flowers bloom atop a stalk as tall as six feet, but its palm-like foliage is only about two feet high. A dramatic plant for beds, it is easy to grow and very hardy.

ZINNIA *(Zinnia):* This annual's handsome flowers come in all colors and sizes. Giant varieties may grow up to three feet high with five-inch blossoms, while miniatures grow tiny bright buttons on twelve-inch plants. Used for borders, beds and for cutting, they bloom into fall if planted in good soil with full sun exposure.

Growing Vegetables

There are no special secrets to a vegetable garden, but there are a few general practices that will help it grow better and faster. The first is to plant a plot only as large as you can handle. A small, well-tended garden will produce more than a larger, neglected garden.

Land cleared of weeds and persistent roots before planting will be much easier to keep weed-free later. If your soil is sandy, add compost or other organic material. Be sure you have an alternate source of water if summer drought is a problem. Fence your garden if pests abound, or if it is close to the woods. Mowing a wide swath around it will help discourage small animals.

Planting times vary with climate and terrain; the best way to learn when to plant various vegetables in your area is to ask a gardening neighbor or your local Cooperative Extension Office. In general, root crops, peas and early greens are planted as soon as the ground can be worked. Squash, cucumber and other fast-growing, but frost-sensitive vegetables are planted about two weeks before the last expected frost. Vegetables started indoors or in greenhouses are transplanted after the danger of frost. In southern and central gardens, many vegetables can be planted directly in the garden, while in the north those same vegetables must be started indoors to have a long enough growing season.

© Lynn Karlin

© Lynn Karlin

© Anita Sabarese

© Lynn Karlin

© Stanley Joseph

© Lynn Karlin

Harvesting Vegetables

While some of us garden for the pure pleasure of working with the soil, for most of us the reward is the harvest. Knowing just when to harvest each vegetable is important. The best rule is that bigger isn't always better. Most vegetables are at their tender, sweet, delicious best when picked quite small. There is no comparison, for example between a succulent, tender zucchini hardly larger than a cigar and the tough, tasteless baseball bats of a week or so later.

Peas should be picked when the pods are firm and deep green, and the peas themselves are firm and round. As the pod matures, the peas lose their flavor as well as their tender texture. Green beans should barely begin to show the bumps of the seeds inside.

Each vegetable has its own peak of perfection, and you will soon begin to recognize these. Remember that picking vegetables encourages new ones to grow, whereas leaving them on the vine to mature causes the plant to stop producing.

Use, refrigerate or preserve vegetables, (see Chapter 3, Preserving the Harvest) soon after picking to retain flavor and nutrients.

© Lynn Karlin

© Lynn Karlin

© Anita Sabarese

C · H · A · P · T · E · R 5

Enjoying the Country Seasons

As springtime flowers and bushes explode with radiant colors, country-goers can't help but be enthralled by nature's new awakening. Wildflowers spring up for children's bouquets. The country spring sun melts all the chills of winter.

Then the sun really comes out. Summer days are filled with country picnics and parties, berry picking and homemade ice-cream. But not every summer day is a lazy day. Summer can be charged with Sunday afternoon picnics and festive country fairs.

The fall brings quieter, more reflective times. You pull those favorite wool sweaters out of the attic and enjoy the brisk air. Fall insures a spectacular display of radiant foliage, and then the leaves drop so youngsters can make fun-filled leaps into the leaf pile. A country fall means baked apples, pumpkin pies, warm breads and a hint of winter.

Winter in the country is perhaps the most festive of the seasons. Along with the holiday cheer, a country winter is filled with family sleigh rides and cross-country skiing expeditions. Winter is a time for building a backyard skating rink, or a big round snowman. Then, it's time to relax with friends over a cup of jasmine tea and some homemade shortbread.

There's nothing like setting a beautiful country table with good wine, home-baked bread and country decorations. Add fresh cut flowers and even if you don't have a spectacular view like this, you'll have a wonderful country celebration.

Spring

Spring is the time for new beginnings, for crocuses blooming through the melting snow, for birds returning to build new nests, for the woods to turn green and the orchards to turn pink and white with blossoms. Even the desert bursts into brilliant bloom.

Flowering trees and shrubs are perhaps the most dramatic of all, since they burst forth with blossoms in just a few days. Even people without an orchard to admire on their hillside can find room for flowering trees and shrubs in their yards.

© Susanna Pashko/Envison

© Grace Davies/Envision

© Rogers Associates

Flowering Trees and Shrubs of Spring

ALMOND *(Prunus dulcis dulcis):* Neat and compact, both flower- and nut-bearing varieties are lovely in blossom. Among the earliest to bloom, they are popular yard trees.

APPLE *(Malus pumula):* Johnny Appleseed is credited with the wide distribution of this tree throughout the temperate zones. Even small yards can have apple blossoms in the spring, and juicy fresh apples in the fall with dwarf and semi-dwarf tree varieties. Crab apple trees, both full sized and the smaller Hopa, grown as an ornamental, have an abundance of blossoms. In a limited space, apple trees may be espaliered against a wall or fence.

CHERRY *(Prunus cerasus):* Sweet, sour and bush varieties provide both fruit and spring bloom. Cherry trees, especially the sour varieties, are smaller and more compact than apple trees, making them fine choices for the small yard. All have white blossoms.

CITRUS *(Citrus):* Grown primarily in the frost-free regions, citrus blossoms are renowned for their sweet fragrance. The flowers bloom most profusely in the spring, but may open at other times of the year as well. Many dwarf citrus trees are available and some, including tangerine and kumquat, are quite small.

DOGWOOD *(Cornus):* One of the most popular flowering trees, dogwood grows in the understory of hardwood forests throughout the eastern half of the United States. Rarely more than forty feet tall, its blossoms are usually white and lie in horizontal layers reminiscent of a Japanese print. The flower is not really a blossom, but two pairs of modified leaves; the true blossom is the tiny cluster in the center of these.

© Anita Sabarese

© Anita Sabarese

FORSYTHIA *(Forsythia):* One of the first bright spots of spring, forsythia's brilliant yellow blossoms cover the entire bush. It is easy to propagate—a single branch pushed into moist soil will take root. If it becomes straggly, it can be pruned back to an orderly shape.

LAUREL *(Rhododendron):* Several varieties of laurel grow in northern and mountain woodlands and are excellent choices for shaded yards. The evergreen foliage is attractive year-round, and the clusters of pink blossoms appear in the spring and early summer.

MAGNOLIA *(Magnolia):* Originally a wild tree of the Deep South, magnolia has become a popular ornamental as far north as Washington, D.C. As a smaller tree it is hardy as far north as central New England. Its large, glossy leaves are attractive, and in the spring it bursts forth in showy pink blossoms.

PEAR *(Pyrus communis):* A favorite of home gardeners, pear trees are small, tidy, compact and thrive on lawns. After the white blossoms fall, the tree is covered with shiny green foliage.

QUINCE *(Cydonia oblonga):* A flowering shrub of compact growth, the quince is best known for its brilliant red blooms and its tart, astringent fruit, which adds needed pectin to fruit jellies.

REDBUD *(Cercis):* Usually fifteen to twenty feet tall, the redbud grows wild from southern New England to Florida and from Nebraska to Mexico. Its bright pink blossoms may appear in the south as early as February.

These flowering trees and shrubs are (moving clockwise from top left) apple, courtesy of Johnny Appleseed; almond, which blooms early; quince, which is a fruit-bearing shrub; and cherry, which is ideal for small yards.

© Anita Sabarese

© Farrell Grehan/FPG International

The Wildflowers Of Childhood

While everyone loves the sight of a field full of wildflowers, they have an especially important place in the hearts of children. For them, flowers are more than things of beauty; they are playthings, craft material, doll food and jewelry.

Wherever honeysuckle grows, children know how to sip its honey. Dandelion fluff is soufflé for dolls' picnics, and with one quick puff, seeded dandelions can be transformed into a cloud of fairy umbrellas. They are also perfect for making wishes or predicting future babies, just as daisies foretell true love. And wild phlox florets can be strung, the tip of one into the center of the next, to make necklaces that are all the more alluring for their fleeting beauty.

A patch of roadside daisies is easy to make into a crown or lei. Cut them with long stems and begin braiding three stems together, adding new flowers to the braid to make a full chain. You should end up with a solid line of blossoms with no stem showing in between. When it is the right length, weave the remaining stem ends into the beginning of the braid to form a circle. When the circle is secure, cut off the ends of the rest of the stems. Crowns can be brought indoors and kept fresh for several days by placing them in a dinner plate full of water. Dry the crown by setting it on a towel before wearing it.

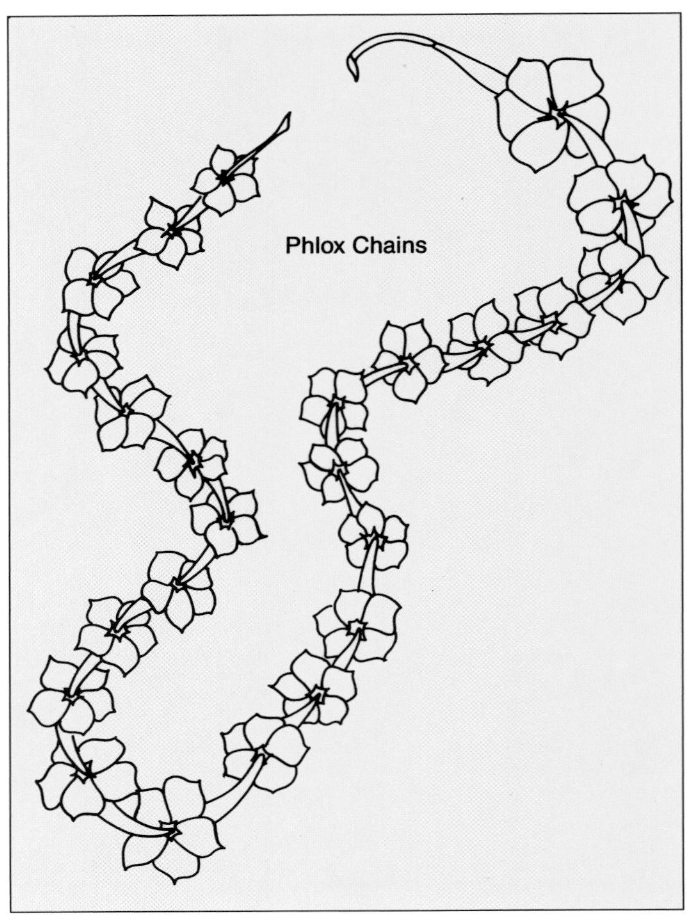

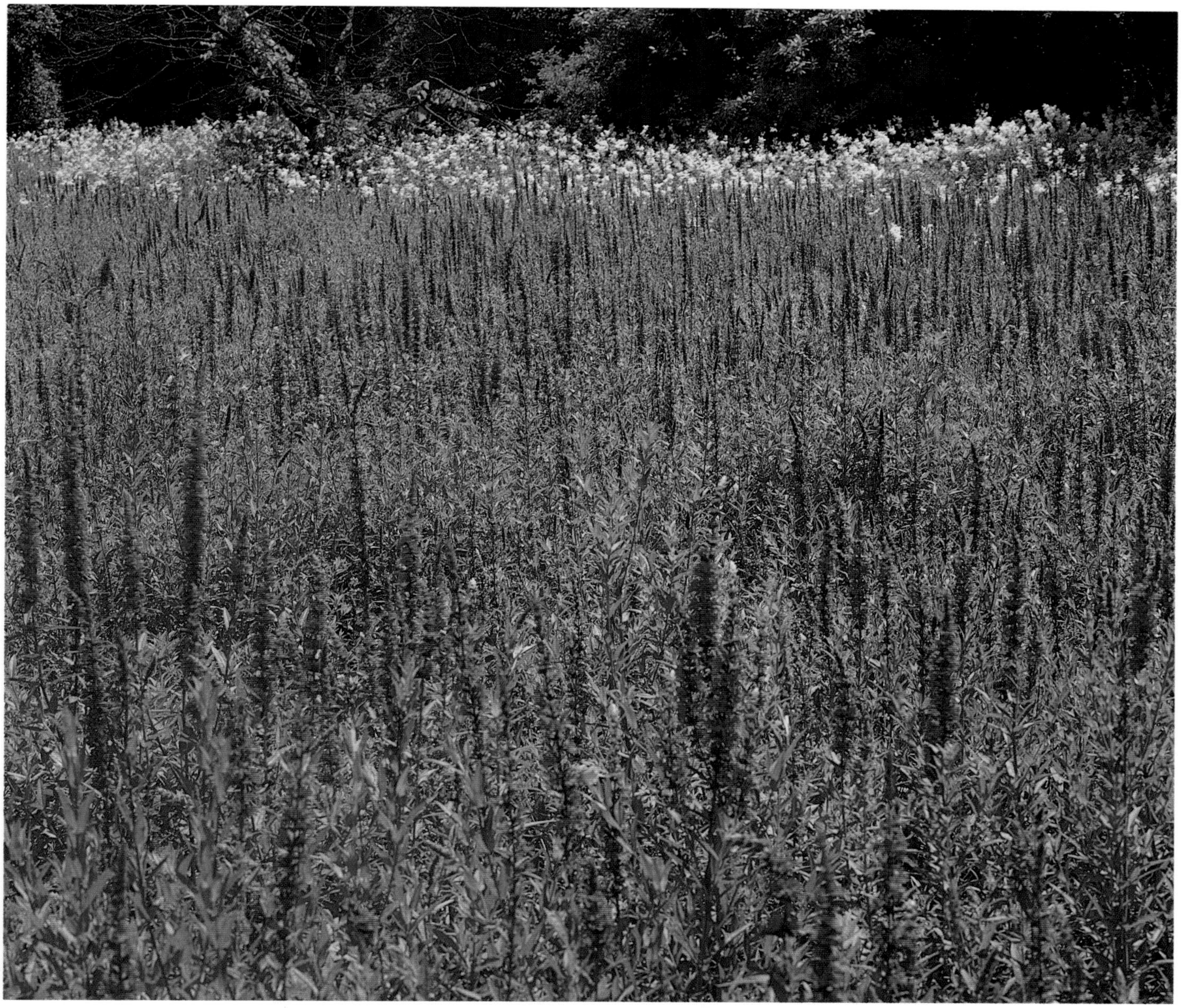

© Dwight Ellefsen/Envision

© Lynn Karlin

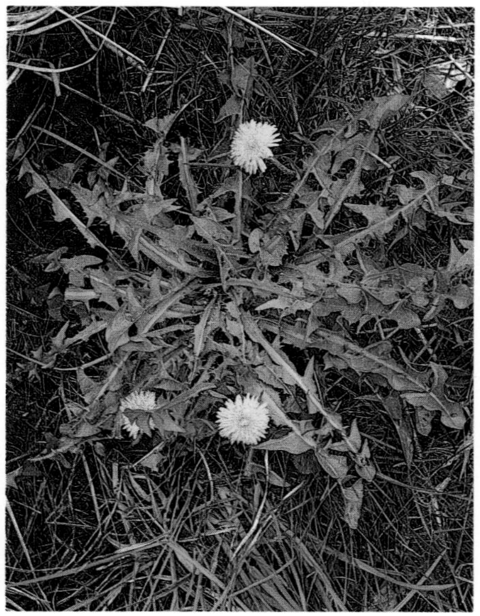

Dandelion Wine

Making wine from the fruits and flowers of the field is a fine old country tradition and the most popular of these is dandelion. Once made by the barrel, it can be made just as successfully in smaller quantities.

2 qts. dandelion blossoms, stems removed
5 lbs. sugar
3 oranges, thinly sliced
3 lemons, thinly sliced
1 tsp. finely cut ginger root (optional)
1 pkg. yeast, dissolved in water

Pour 4 quarts of boiling water over the dandelion blossoms, and let stand 3 days, stirring each day. Strain the liquid and add the sugar, sliced oranges, sliced lemons, ginger root, if desired, and the yeast. Let stand 3 days, stirring each day. Skim out the fruit and let stand at least 4 weeks. Strain through a cheesecloth, then bottle and cap. Dandelion wine tastes best if aged for at least 6 months.

Makes 4 quarts.

Spring Greens

Spring greens are available in nearly every part of North America, and grow in large fields and wildlands as well as in small plots of land. Even a lawn or garden will probably yield a few of the most popular edible greens—and the owner will be glad to get rid of these troublesome weeds that taste so good.

The only trick to gathering greens is to get them while they are young, tender and sweet. The most popular of all are dandelion greens, which must be picked before the flower stem emerges, and are at their very sweetest when only a few inches long. At this size they make a tender, delicious salad when tossed with vinegar and oil and a hint of mustard. Whole cherry tomatoes make a beautiful and delicious contrast. As a cooked green dandelion greens are frequently tossed with crumbled bacon.

Poke is a well-loved green with a history. Early explorers were so impressed with it that they carried home its seeds. It is still a popular cultivated green in Europe and North Africa. To gather poke, look early in the spring for the old, dried stalks of last year's plants. New shoots grow from the same root and should be picked as tiny, tender 6-inch sprouts with their leaves still curled tight. Parboil the greens for 10 minutes in plenty of water, then drain and cook slowly in a little water and olive oil (or bacon drippings) for at least 20 minutes.

There are many other plants that furnish tasty and highly nutritious spring greens, but local names and varieties vary greatly. The best way to learn which are plentiful in your locality is to ask neighbors, especially those who grew up there.

Easter Eggs

In Pennsylvania Dutch country as well as in other rural areas, eggs are dyed with natural plant colors and decorated by scratching designs on them. The dye will scratch off with the point of a heavy needle, leaving a design etched in white.

Another decorating method involves reverse stenciling with leaves or flowers during the dyeing process. Neither of these is difficult to do and the latter requires no artistic ability at all.

The outer skins of onions make an excellent yellow-orange dye, and other vegetables such as chopped beets, carrot tops (greens), grape juice, blackberries and blueberries also make good dyes. Simply boil these in water until the color shows a strong dye, add a little vinegar and put in the eggs. The longer you leave them, the deeper the color will be. To make a scratched design, work as soon as possible after removing them from the dye.

For stenciled designs, find small leaves, especially lacy ones such as yarrow, ferns, carrot tops or other foliage with a nice shape. Place these on the eggshell where you want the design to be. Carefully wrap the egg in a single layer of nylon stocking to hold the plant firmly in place. Dip the egg in the dye until you've achieved the desired color, rinse it in clear water, then unwrap it.

You can also make beautiful designs by cutting tiny rows of paper dolls from waxed paper and wrapping them around the center of the egg, or by cutting tiny waxed paper snowflakes and placing them on the egg at random. Wrap the egg in a nylon stocking as you would with stenciled designs. The wax helps prevent the dye from penetrating the covered area.

May Day

A country festival which dates to pagan times, May Day is a joyous, spontaneous celebration of the arrival of spring. Garlands of flowers are woven to decorate churches or to carry in parades and are often made into crowns for the Queen of the May. The Morris Dancers—who originated centuries ago in the English midlands and dress in traditional white suits with bells on their ankles—are often a part of these springtime festivities, a custom recently revived in the United States, where groups have formed in a number of communities.

One of England's best known May Day traditions is the gathering of the choristers from the Magdalen Choir School in the tower at Oxford at 6 a.m. to sing *Te Deum Patrem Colimus* and other Latin hymns to the silent crowd gathered on the bridge and in boats on the river below.

Maypoles began as symbols of the flowering tree, yet they vary with local traditions: a 134-foot-tall pole was once erected on London's Strand, but smaller ones are still found in towns and villages throughout England and even occasionally in the United States and Canada. Girls dance around the pole, each holding a streamer. As they dance in and out, the streamers braid down the length of the pole to form a pattern.

Today, centuries after the first maypole celebration, children and adults still enjoy celebrating the arrival of May, and with it, the promise of summer's bounty.

May Baskets

May baskets evolved from the practice of decorating the doors of neighboring houses with fresh-cut flowering branches or laying little nosegays of spring flowers on doorsteps on the first of May.

Today, the May basket is a charming country custom for children, who present adults with little baskets on the morning of the first of May. Traditionally, these are filled with fresh wildflowers, but other small remembrances are also used, such as homemade candy, small cookies, a jar of jelly or a sachet of potpourri.

The baskets are quite small and usually decorated with pastel flowers such as violets. A paper cup makes a perfect base to decorate as a May basket, but small boxes can also be used. Cut tissue or crepe paper first into strips, then into petal shapes and wrap around a cup. The petals will frame the upper rim.

For even fancier May baskets, cut crepe paper into 4-inch strips of petals and roll the top edges over a small, round object such as a knitting needle. Push the rolled paper to the center from each end to wrinkle it, and hold the shape before removing the knitting needle. Do this twice on each petal (see illustration), to form a point with the two rolled edges. The petals make the basket look like a rose.

Since May baskets are a surprise, children hang them on a neighbor's doorknob, then ring the doorbell and run to hide.

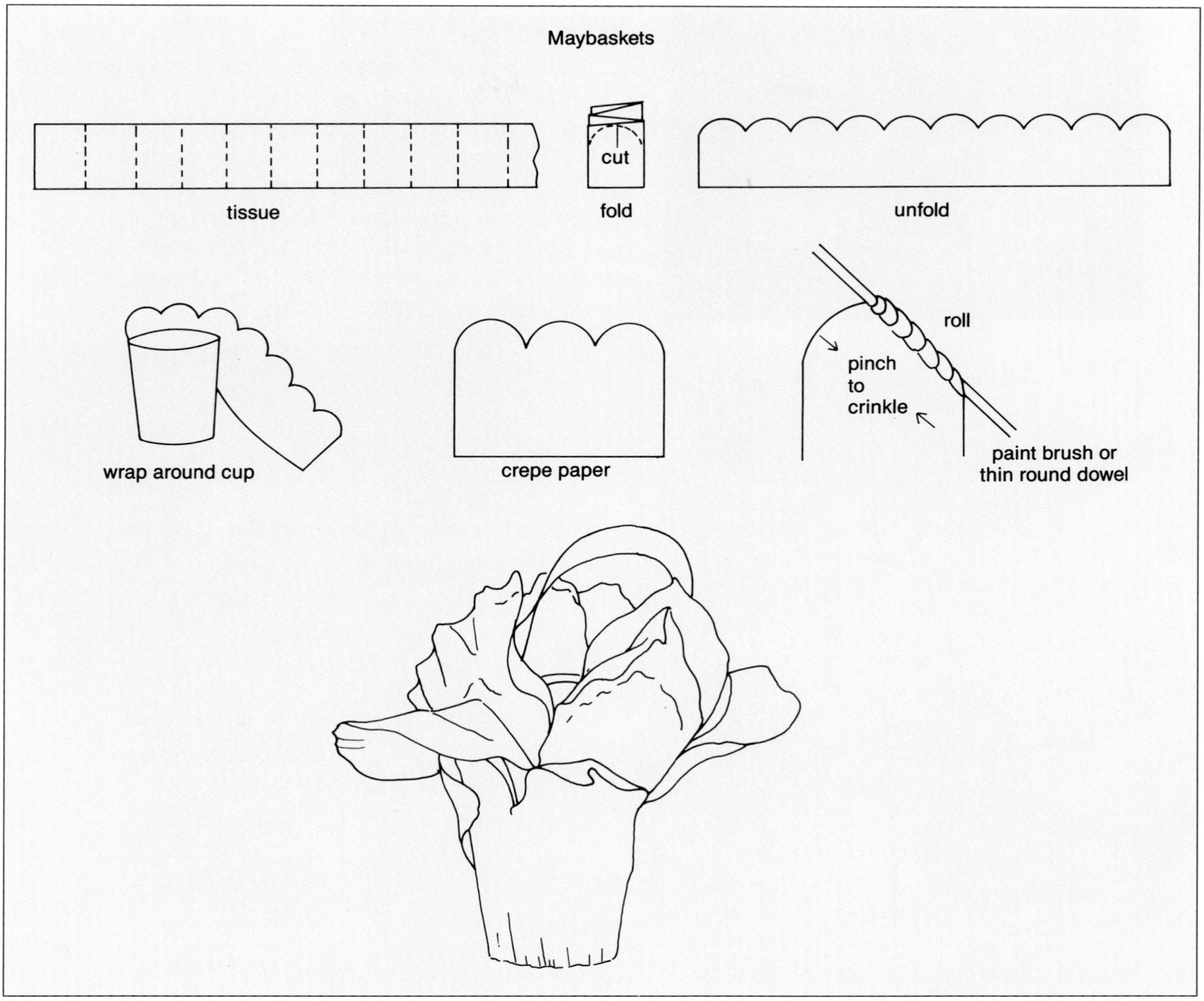

Maybaskets

tissue

cut

fold

unfold

wrap around cup

crepe paper

roll

pinch
to
crinkle

paint brush or
thin round dowel

© Mike Holley/Envision

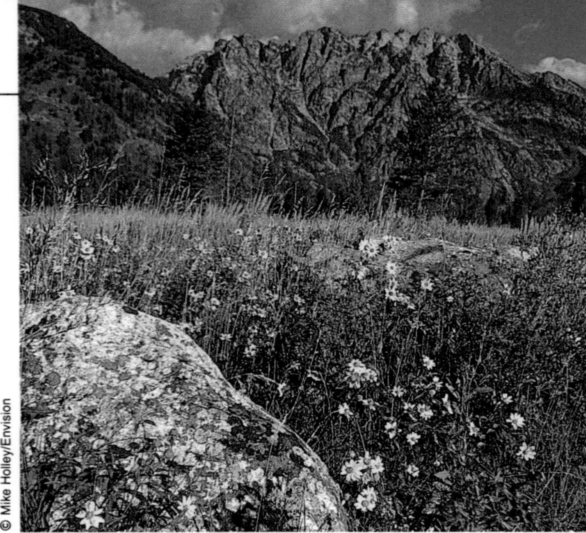

Summer

Summer in the country is a time for relaxation. It is a time to sit on the porch with a frosty glass of sun tea and watch the bees and hummingbirds work. The scents of a country summer are rich and heady, like freshly mown hay, flowers and smoke from a campfire. Its colors are green and gold under a rich blue sky, muted at the edges with summer haze. Summer is a time to enjoy the rewards of country living.

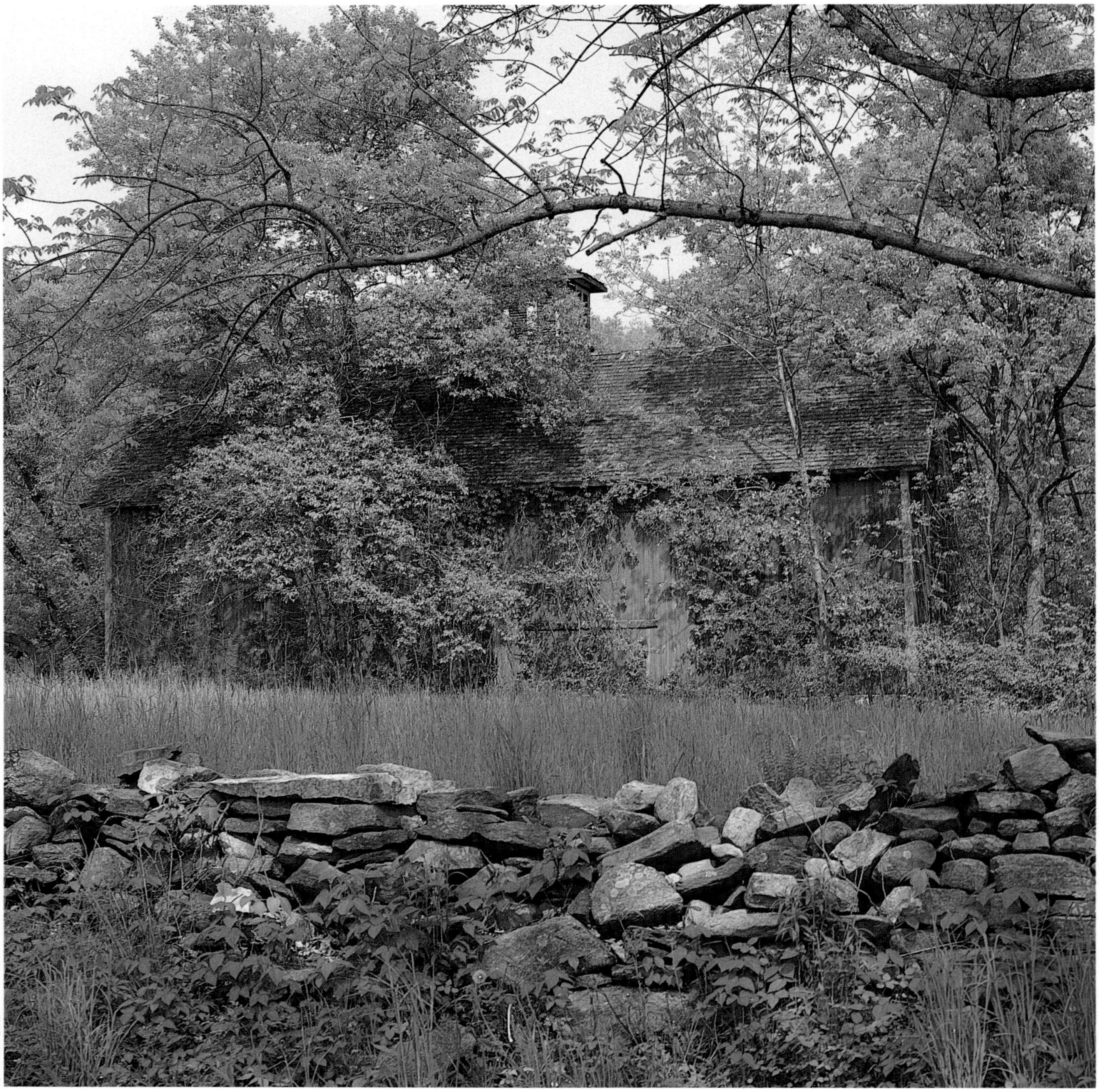

© William Seitz

© William Seitz

SUN TEA

On a warm sunny day you can make delicious tea in the sun that will not cloud when stored in the refrigerator, as ordinary tea does.

Fill a clear glass jar with cold water. Add a teaspoonful of tea for each cup of water. Add fresh mint, lemon balm or beebalm leaves, or slices of fresh lemon if desired. Shake well and place the jar outdoors in the sun. As the sun warms the water, you will see the color of the tea leaves disperse. Depending on the strength of the sun and the size of the jar, your tea may be ready in as little as 2 hours. Chill well. Pour through a strainer into tall glasses filled with ice. During a hot spell, make a jar in advance each day to chill overnight for the next day.

© Gordon E. Smith 1988

Blueberry Picking

The most accommodating of berries, the blueberry grows in the open, on bushes without thorns that are sometimes high enough to harvest without bending over. Their neat packaging protects them from being crushed and helps them stay fresh longer after picking. In some areas they ripen all at once and can be raked from the bushes in great numbers instead of being picked one at a time. *And* they are delicious and versatile.

While it is hard to beat a good wild blueberry pie, close contenders are cobbler and its variations, known by such original names as fool, grunt and buckle. Each of these pies has a different topping.

Blueberry Grunt

4 c. blueberries
1/2 to 1 c. sugar
1/4 tsp. cinnamon
nutmeg

In a 9-inch square pan, place blueberries, sugar, cinnamon and a few grindings of nutmeg. Spread shortcake or biscuit dough over this to form a top.

Bake at 400°F until the top is well-browned and the berries bubbly. Cut into squares and serve hot.

Makes nine squares.

Blueberry Muffins

1/4 c. butter
1/4 c. sugar
1 egg, beaten
2 c. flour
4 tsp. baking powder
1/2 tsp. salt
1 c. milk
2 c. blueberries

Cream butter and sugar. Add a beaten egg and mix well. Sift in the flour, baking powder and salt, alternating with the milk. Mix well, but do not beat. The batter should be a little lumpy. Fold in the blueberries and spoon the batter into greased muffin tins, filling each cup only half full. Bake at 375°F for 30 minutes or until evenly browned.

Makes 12 muffins.

Blackberry Picking

Blackberry picking, unlike the more genteel art of blueberry gathering, is not a pleasant little foray to the edge of the meadow with a pail swinging alongside. At best, it's an encounter with nature, at worst, it's a full scale battle.

Blackberries grow in dense thickets of vines so covered with thorns that a few moments of unprotected combat leaves one looking like the loser in a cat fight. It's not the place for shorts and sandals —full medieval armor might be more appropriate.

The first thing to do is skirt the thicket and pick all the berries you can easily reach. This will usually give you about half the amount needed for any recipe; your half-full pail will give you the incentive to go on.

Look for the best spots—those where you can see the most ripe berries—and make paths directly to these. While a machete would help, garden clippers can do a pretty good job. Wearing garden gloves, cut the dead canes and any live ones that you've cleaned of berries. Those will die over the winter, and next year's berries will be born on the green, tender looking canes of this year's new growth. Separate the new canes and use their thorns to attach them to neighboring vines out of your way.

As for the rewards of your labors, the first bite of a lucious juicy blackberry pie is reward enough for many hours of hard picking.

© Jerry Howard/Positive Images

Claire's Blackberry Pie

piecrust pastry
2 tbsp. flour
3/4 c. plus 1 tbsp. sugar
3 c. ripe blackberries
1/4 c. minute tapioca
1 tsp. lemon juice

Line a 9-inch pie plate with pastry. Sprinkle with the flour and 1 tablespoon of sugar. Add ripe blackberries and sprinkle with tapioca, lemon juice and the remaining sugar (a full cup if some of the berries are under-ripe). Cover with a pastry crust, crimp edges and cut steam vents. Bake at 425°F about 45 minutes, or until nicely browned.

© Gary Mottau/Positive Images

© Steven Mark Needham/Envision

Ice Cream

We've come a long way from the old hand-cranked freezer, past an electrically run one and into the era of an iceless, saltless canister that's stored in the freezer between uses, and needs only an occasional turn of the handle. We'll leave it to the experts to discuss the relative merits of each product, and concentrate on the recipes instead.

Some ice creams are simply cream, sweetening and fruit or other flavoring. Others begin with an egg custard mixture, which makes a richer ice cream. Ice milks and sherbets are made with milk in varying amounts or with no milk at all, depending on the flavor.

The procedure is essentially the same, whether the freezer is hand or electrically operated. Fill the canister half full with the cream mixture and pack layers of crushed ice and salt into the drum around it. Keep the dasher in the canister moving as the mixture freezes. When it will no longer turn, remove the dasher and return the canister to the drum to finish off the ice cream. The newer types are even easier; their distinct advantage is that you can make the ice cream for dessert as you eat dinner.

These recipes work in any type of ice-cream maker, but you may need to make smaller amounts for the freezer-type canisters.

© Grace Davies/Envision

APPLESAUCE ICE CREAM

1 c. light cream
1 1/2 c. sour cream
1 pt. homemade, unstrained applesauce
1/2 c. sugar

Mix light cream with sour cream and sugar. Freeze until it begins to thicken, then add applesauce and continue freezing.

PEACH ICE CREAM

This same recipe can be used with any fruit, but the amount of sugar may need to be adjusted to compensate for the acidity of different fruits. Try pureéd blackberries, strawberries or pineapple.

1 c. sugar
1 tbsp. lemon juice
2 c. mashed fresh peaches
1 qt. heavy cream
optional: 1 tsp. chopped, candied ginger

In a large bowl, sprinkle sugar and lemon juice over the mashed fresh peaches. Let this stand for 30 minutes and add the heavy cream. Freeze according to the directions for your freezer. A teaspoon of chopped, candied ginger can be added for extra zest after the first 10 minutes of freezing.

LEMON ICE CREAM

This ice cream is rich and delicious and just slightly tart.

2 c. milk
2 c. cream
2 c. sugar
juice of 4 lemons
1 lemon rind, grated

Combine the milk and cream and mix in the sugar, stirring until it dissolves. Using a wire whisk, slowly stir the lemon juice into the cream mixture. Freeze the mixture for about 10 minutes, then add the grated rind of a lemon. Continue freezing until the ice cream is ready. Note: The lemon juice will make the cream thicken but not curdle it if it is added slowly and stirred in vigorously.

© William Seitz

Picnics

A picnic is not just a meal eaten out-of-doors, and it's more than a collection of foods that can be packed in a cooler and eaten in transit. A good picnic requires some planning; it is a well conceived and balanced meal. But it doesn't have to be a pretentious or complicated one.

The methods of packing, preserving and serving the food need to be considered carefully, and recipes chosen accordingly. Fussy or fragile foods are best served in the dining room, along with dishes that require a lot of last-minute attention. The length of time between refrigerator and serving will govern the menu somewhat.

Self-contained foods are especially nice for picnics: those "packaged" dishes such as calzones or samosas, main-dish turnovers filled with ingredients that are good at any temperature.

Everything does not have to be prepared ahead of time. A smorgasbord in which the hostess provides a wide assortment of fixings and everyone participates in the do-it-yourself creation of sandwiches has one big advantage—the menu will please everyone.

The selection might include any or all of the following: cold meats, including salami, pepperoni, bologna, roast beef, turkey or chicken, ham, cooked bacon, smoked salmon and sardines; cheeses such as provolone, Gruyère, Cheddar and Munster, all sliced, as well as cream cheese and feta. Vegetables should include leaf lettuce, sliced tomatoes, slivered peppers, sliced onions, sliced cucumbers, sliced avocado (tossed with lemon juice to keep it from turning brown, or cut at serving time) and dill pickles sliced lengthwise. Most of these can be arranged on plates that can be covered in plastic wrap and stacked in the cooler.

Breads can include white, whole wheat, rye, pumpernickel and Italian rolls. Spreads should be mayonnaise, butter, horseradish, Italian dressing and several mustards from mild to hot. Pickles, olives, roasted peppers in oil, sprigs of fresh herbs and other garnishes add a nice touch.

© William Seitz

© William Seitz

Calzone

1/2 lb. Italian salami or pepperoni
1/2 lb. mozzarella cheese
oregano
pepper
calzone dough (see recipe, below)

Roll and stretch pizza dough as thin as possible on a floured surface and cut into 4-inch rounds with a biscuit cutter. Cut cheese and salami into thin strips and place a heaping teaspoonful on each circle of dough. Sprinkle with oregano and pepper. Brush edges with water and fold dough over to make a half-circle. Seal with a fork. Bake at 350°F until golden, about 15 minutes. Cool and store in the refrigerator, but allow to come to room temperature before serving.

Makes 2 to 3 dozen calzones.

Calzone Dough

1 pkg. dry yeast
1 c. lukewarm water
1 1/2 tsp. sugar
2 1/2 to 3 c. flour
1 1/2 tsp. salt
3 tbsp. vegetable oil

Sprinkle yeast over warm water and add sugar. Stir lightly and let stand 5 minutes. Mix 1 cup of flour with salt in a large bowl and add the yeast mixture and oil. Beat well until smooth, then add flour gradually, mixing well after each addition. Use enough flour to make a soft dough. Turn out onto a surface dusted with flour and knead about 10 minutes. Place dough in an oiled bowl and turn once to coat dough. Cover and let rise until it doubles in bulk—about an hour in a 65° room, less if it's warmer. Punch down and knead very lightly for about a minute before using.

Makes approximately enough dough for 2 to 3 dozen calzones.

Tomato And Mozzarella Salad

Alternate slices of mozzarella cheese with thick slices of peeled tomatoes in a dish. Pour over this a dressing made of olive oil and red wine vinegar and sprinkle with chopped fresh chives and oregano.

Hot Wings

1/3 c. yellow cornmeal
1/3 c. white flour
1 1/2 tsp. chili powder
1/2 tsp. cayenne pepper
1/2 tsp. salt
3 lb. chicken wings

Combine cornmeal, flour and spices in a small paper bag. Separate the wings at the joints and save the tips for soup. Toss the wings gently in the bag and lay them on a lightly oiled cookie sheet, leaving a little space between them. Bake for about an hour at 375°F. These can be covered with foil and carried warm, wrapped in a towel, if the picnic site is not far, or cooled, chilled and served cold. A jalapeño or Mexican-style tomato sauce makes a good dip for hot wings.

Makes approximately 6 servings.

White Bean Salad

4 tbsp. olive oil
2 tbsp. wine vinegar
1 clove garlic, mashed
2 cans Italian white beans, rinsed and drained
2 tomatoes, chopped
1/2 c. pitted black olives, sliced
4 sprigs fresh parsley, chopped

Whisk oil, vinegar and garlic together in a bowl. Add remaining ingredients, toss gently and leave to marinate several hours in the refrigerator.

Makes about 5 cups of salad.

Campfire Cooking

Campfires are not just for toasting marshmallows and grilling hot dogs. The campfire is the center of life at the campsite, where everyone gathers to talk and tell stories. It is warmth on a chilly August morning, a welcoming flame in the dark of night. And all day long it's a hot-water heater, clothes dryer and, most of all, a cookstove.

Cooking on a campfire may take a little practice. Because you cook on it, in it, under it and in front of it, it's a whole new world of cooking, but the same principles you learned about cooking indoors on a woodstove prevail outdoors, too. You have to learn to regulate the heat the best you can, and adjust your cooking to it when you can't. Expect a little smoke in your eyes and a kink in your back as you bend over to stir and turn dinner. But remember that whatever you cook will be eaten ravenously, since everyone's appetite is enormous when eating out-of-doors, even if the campfire is in your own backyard.

Do not use your best cooking utensils for a campfire and never use those with wooden or plastic handles. Cast iron is best because it holds heat evenly. Aluminum foil may not be what the Native Americans used, but they probably would have if it had been available. A reflector oven lends an air of magic to the cooking art.

The novice campfire cook should begin with things that are broiled, roasted or toasted. Look for recipes that involve spearing meat on skewers, and let the fire burn down to hot coals before grilling over it. Anything you would broil on a backyard grill—chicken, sausage, fish—can be done on a campfire, but it will taste even better because you are cooking it over wood.

Potatoes and corn are especially fun for children because they cook right in the fire. Wash potatoes and wrap them in a double layer of foil. Once the coals are glowing, nestle the potatoes right into them, and turn the potatoes frequently so that all sides are cooked. Check one after about half an hour to see if it is done. To cook corn, pull back the husks, remove the silk and rewrap the ears in the husks. Put the whole ears in a bucket of water to moisten them thoroughly, then wrap them in foil. You can put these right into the coals like the potatoes or cook them on the grate over the fire. Check them after about ten minutes if they are in the coals; fifteen minutes if they are over the fire.

Reflector ovens are easy to use and you can watch the progress in these more easily than in your oven at home. You can buy reflector ovens at any camping supply store. They stand in front of the fire and rely on the simple principle that a shiny metal surface reflects heat. With one sheet above and one sheet below at 90-degree angles, the heat is concentrated on whatever is in the middle. You can bake chicken, biscuits, cakes and cobblers this way and everyone will love to watch them cook.

© William Seitz

Clambake

While Narragansett Bay, Massachusetts, residents claim that their rock-bound coast was home to the first clambake long before the Europeans arrived, coastal residents from Eastport, Maine, to Block Island, Rhode Island, dispute that claim.
But nearly everyone agrees that clambakes began somewhere in New England or the Maritime Provinces, in a day when lobster was far more plentiful.

The details and the location may vary, but the essentials of a clambake remain much the same. A hole is dug in the sand, well above the high-tide line; it is filled with nonporous rocks and a fire is built over the rocks. After it has burned for several hours, the fire is raked away and the hot stones are covered with wet seaweed. Lobster, clams, corn and potatoes are quickly placed over this and covered with more seaweed. The entire thing is finally covered with a canvas tarp soaked in sea water and anchored around the edges with stones.

Sometimes clam chowder is served while this delicious mélange steams in wet seaweed for about an hour. Then someone melts butter, and everything comes out of the pit and is served at the same time.

In places where the shore is too rocky to dig a hole in the sand, a good depression in the rocks works just as well. You can vary the menu by adding chicken to the seafood and vegetables. (Coastal natives consider this an abomination best left to people who live inland.)

To make retrieval easier, the clams and potatoes are usually tied in squares of cheesecloth. This is especially useful for a big crowd, where each person's cheesecloth square is filled with clams, lobsters, potatoes and corn. Another advantage to this is that everyone can be served while all of the food is piping hot.

The corn should be prepared by peeling back its husks and removing the silk, then wrapping it back in the husks. These natural wrappings give the corn an incomparable flavor.

Dessert may vary with the place and the season, but ice cold watermelon is common. In Maine in August, dessert may be blueberry pie or blackberry buckle, baked in reflector ovens in front of the fire as the rocks are heating.

© R. Rowan/FPG International

© Joe Viesti/Viesti Associates, Inc.

County Fairs

County fairs are in the rich tradition of the British countryside. Villagers gathered at the fairs to relax after the season's chores, count their blessings and compare their harvests.

Today, we still take our clearest jellies and biggest vegetables to fair to be compared and judged, while we watch the 4-H kids brush and trim their prize-winning sheep.

To locate county fairs and other harvest festivals in your area or one you plan to visit, contact the County Cooperative Extension office. They are in charge of 4-H, and wherever there's a fair, 4-H members will be in the middle of it!

© Joe Viesti/Viesti Associates, Inc.

© Joe Viesti/Viesti Associates, Inc.

© Joe Viesti/Viesti Associates, Inc.

© Joe Viesti/Viesti Associates, Inc.

© Jerry Howard/Positive Images

Fall Bounty

Fall is the season of homecoming, of drawing closer before winter, of gathering in the rewards of summer's kindness. Gleaming jars of preserves, the tangy smell of simmering pickles mingled with wood stove smoke on the first frosty morning—in fall all of this is set against a backdrop of magnificent blazing maples, red oaks and golden birches. The crisp autumn air beckons and urges you outdoors to gather dried flowers, or take a country drive in search of just the right pumpkin for the jack–o'–lantern.

© William Seitz

© Anita Sabarese

Wild Weeds for Fall Bouquets

The woods and fields of autumn are full of grasses, weeds and seeds that can be combined into stunning dried arrangements for the country home. Harvesting them is easy, and since nature has already dried them for you, they need no special care or treatment before you use them.

Each landscape offers its own treasures, which you will quickly spot as you walk through gardens, fields and woodland paths or drive along country roads. Even vacant lots and parks in the city offer a variety. Here are some of the most common ones.

© Tony Cenicola

© Anita Sabarese

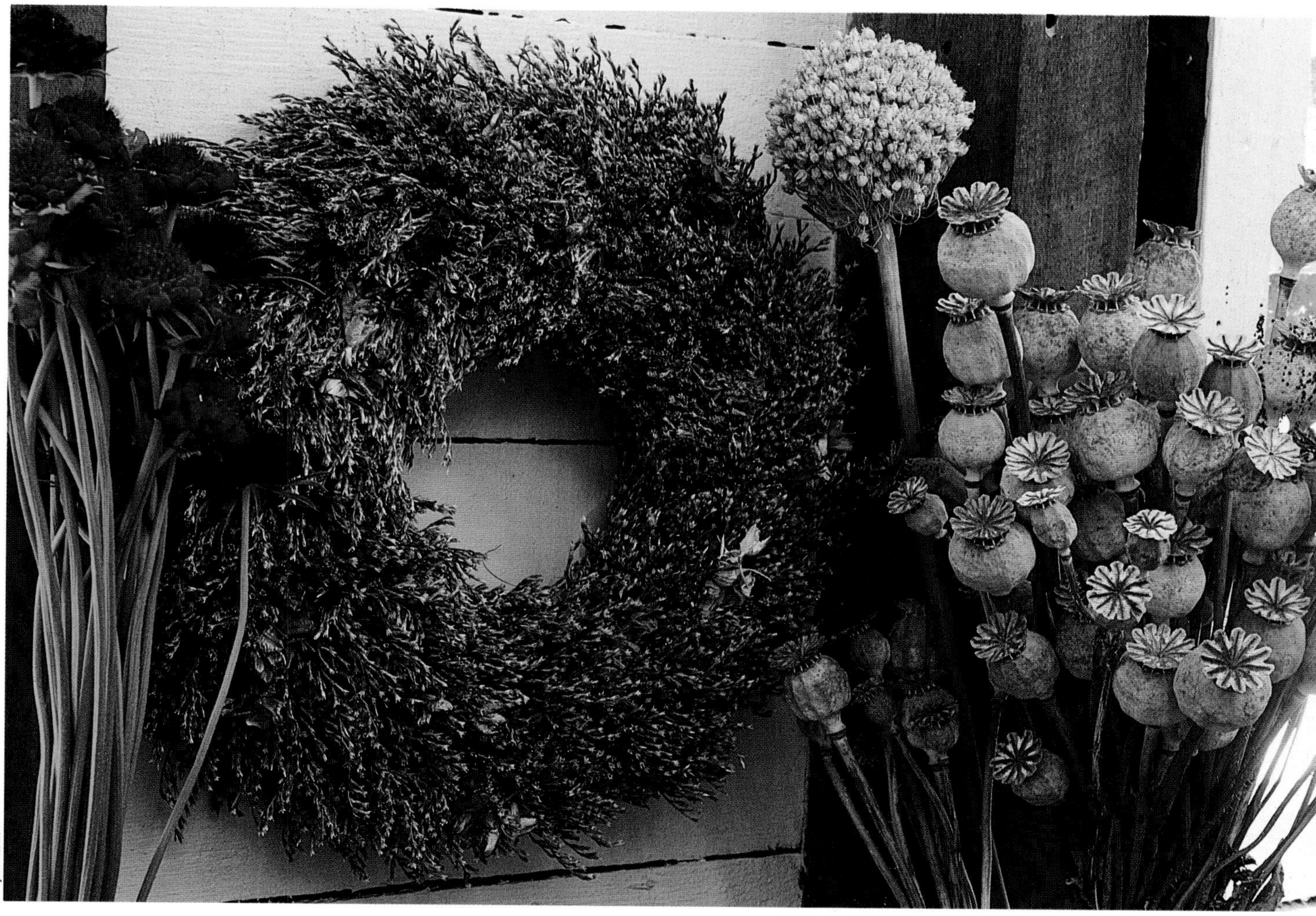

© Lynn Karlin

© Francois Dillschneider/FPG International

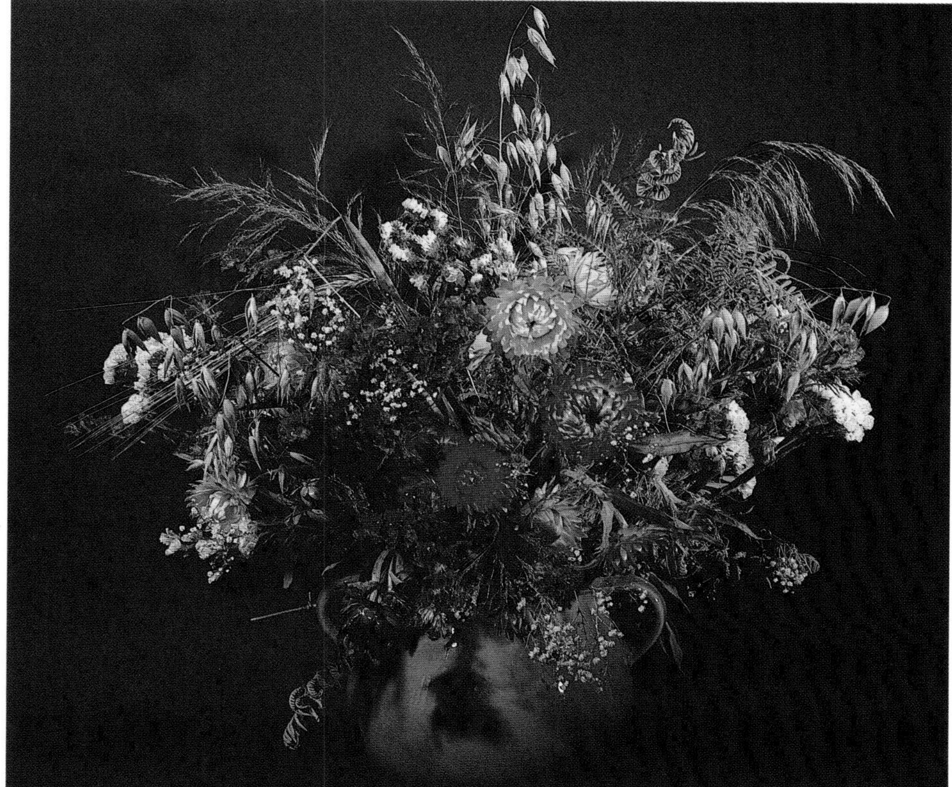

AGRIMONY *(Agrimonia eupatoria):* Look for the spikes of firm brown seedpods of this plant in the herb garden. It provides a good accent, or it may be placed fanlike as the background of a more formal arrangement.

BEE BALM *(Monarda didyma):* Look in the herb garden or in the wild for these buttonlike pompons. Good in arrangements or on wreaths, they can also be used as natural needle-holders for the short stems of smaller dried flowers in miniature arrangements.

DILL *(Anethum graveolens):* If a few seed heads make it through the pickling season, save them for their wide clusters of seeds held on umbrella-like stems. They are fragile, but even if the seeds fall off, they are still attractive.

DOCK *(Rumex):* One of the most common roadside weeds, and one of the few that can be gathered year round in snowy climates. The tall, sturdy spikes of dock are often visible above the snow.

EVENING PRIMROSE *(Oenethera biennis):* Long clusters of tulip-shaped seedpods with outward turned "petals" form after the primrose flowers fall. They look like little flowers carved from wood.

FALSE INDIGO *(Baptisia):* Large clumps of this plant may be found in flower gardens, where its large, almost black seeds will attract notice at once.

HOLLYHOCK *(Alcea rosea):* The perennial bed may yield tall stems of brown buttons left from hollyhock blossoms. These are particularly attractive on cone wreaths.

JIMSON WEED *(Datura stramonium):* Common in waste areas, such as vacant lots and roadsides throughout North America, the prickly brown seedpods of jimson weed are useful in both arrangements and wreaths.

MEADOW SWEET *(Filipendula):* Tall, dark brown spikes stand out above the fall foliage of this common field and roadside shrub. The smaller side shoots are good for miniature arrangements.

Windblown pampas grass (left) and wheat actually shimmer in the summer sun. Pampas grass is often used as a landscaping accent, and wheat is good for dried flower arrangements.

MILKWEED *(Asclepias):* Found along roadsides in most of North America, the pods of milkweed and its smaller relative, butterfly weed, are good for large arrangements or as frames for miniature dried arrangements.

PAMPAS GRASS *(Cortaderia selloana):* This tall, handsome grass with its silver plumes is used as a landscaping accent.

QUEEN ANNE'S LACE *(Daucus carota):* As the flower fades, it forms nestlike seed heads. This wild relative of the carrot can be found throughout much of North America.

RABBIT TAIL GRASS *(Lagurus oratus):* These fluffy seed heads, which can be two inches in diameter, give an unexpected soft texture to fall bouquets. Look for this grass on the West Coast.

SCARLET SUMAC *(Rhus):* Dark red spires of this fruit are easily spotted along roadsides and in places with poor, sandy soil throughout the east.

SHEPHERD'S PURSE *(Capsella bursa-pastoris):* This annual "weed" is found in gardens, vacant lots, roadsides and even sidewalk verges. Its feathery stem and flat seedpods are surprisingly strong. You might want to use these to support other less sturdy plants in an arrangement.

TEASEL *(Dipsacus radicans):* The pale tan thistlelike heads of teasel are framed in narrow curling bracts. Be careful of this plant: the thistles are very prickly.

TRUMPETVINE *(Campsis radicans):* The long thin seedpods of this vine will usually be found clinging to walls, porches or trellises where it is planted for its bright orange flowers.

WHEAT *(Triticum aestivum):* Along with rye, oats and other grains, wheat is often found at the edges of fields where it has escaped the harvest. Rye is often used as a roadside planting after new road construction since it germinates quickly and holds soil well.

© Nancy Hill

© Jerry Howard/Positive Images

Cornhusk Decorations

Cornhusks make attractive harvest wreaths, but be sure to dry the husks first, then soak them in water to soften before you begin working. Husks can be braided or split into 2-inch-wide strips and knotted onto a wire wreath frame. Use a single-wire frame and knot husks by folding them in half lengthwise and bringing the two ends around the

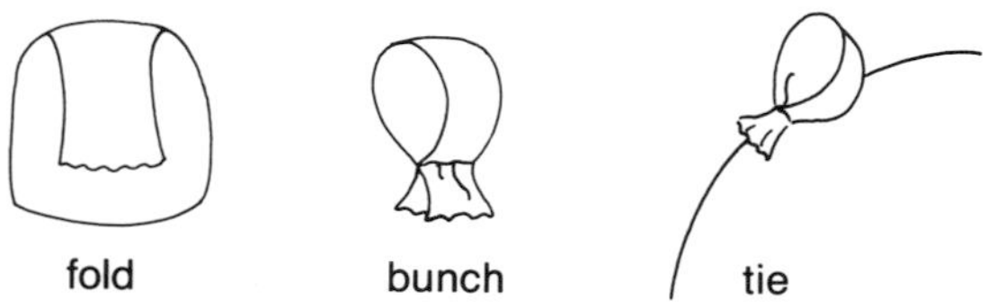

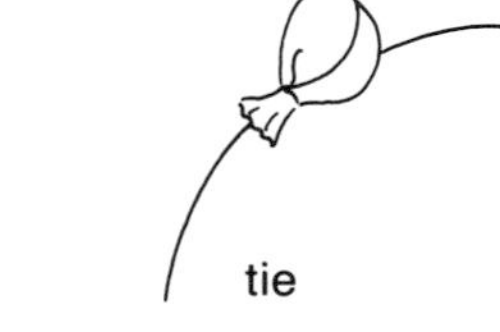

wire and through the loop. Pull tight and continue until the ring is full. On large frames, alternate the tails inward and outward to make a fuller wreath.

These can be decorated with cornhusk flowers. To make them, cut husks into petal shapes and wrap clusters of them on wire or natural plant stems, tying with fine wire, raffia or thread. Spread the petals as the husks dry to form a natural shape.

Or split 3- or 4-inch lengths of husk into thin strips almost to the base to form a fringe. Wrap these around a stem and secure them with wire or thread. They will curl as they dry. You can make them curl tighter by wrapping them around pencils and tying them with thread. When they are dry, remove the pencils and thread and separate the curls.

Tulip shapes, poppies, daisies, even daffodils, can be created by combining these methods. These flowers can decorate cornhusk wreaths, or be arranged in baskets or used in dried arrangements.

© Wanda La Rock/Envision

Apple Picking

On a crisp day in late September, when the hillsides are ablaze with color and the sky is a deep, rich blue, it's time for the whole family to don sweaters, pack some bushel baskets in the back of the car and head for the nearest apple orchard.

Having selected a tree full of apples of the right variety, you need to approach it with some organization. Someone nimble and well balanced should climb the tree and choose a limb. The rest of the group should stand away from the tree as the limb is shaken gently, watching where the apples fall. After a few have fallen, gather the apples. The rule is to avoid bruising the fruit whenever possible.

Stop for fresh cider on the way home and plan what to do with the bounty in the back of the station wagon.

© William Seitz

© William Seitz

© Glenn R. Steiner/FPG International

APPLE PIE

piecrust pastry
1 1/2 tsp. flour
6 c. sliced apples
3/4 c. sugar
1/2 tsp. nutmeg
1/4 tsp. cloves
1/4 tsp. cinnamon
1/4 tsp. salt
milk

Sprinkle half the flour in the bottom of a pastry-lined 9-inch pie tin and spread the apples, as closely as possible, in layers to half fill the tin. In a bowl, mix the sugar and spices together with the salt and the rest of the flour and sprinkle half of this mixture on the apples. Repeat with the remaining apples and the sugar mixture. Cover with pastry, crimp edges to seal and cut steam vents. Brush pie with milk. Bake at 450°F for 15 minutes, then at 350°F for 30 to 45 minutes longer, until the crust is golden.

For a fancy touch, cut circles from the extra piecrust pastry, using a small cookie cutter. Cut two leaves for each circle and several short narrow strips. Arrange these on top of the pie to look like apples with leaves and stems. Brush apples and leaves with milk and bake pie.

APPLE MUFFINS

2 c. sifted flour
1/2 c. sugar
3/4 tsp. salt
1 tbsp. baking powder
1 tsp. cinnamon
1/2 tsp. nutmeg
1 egg, well beaten
1 1/4 c. milk
1/4 c. melted shortening
1 1/2 tsp. lemon juice
1 1/4 c. finely chopped apples

Combine the dry ingredients in a bowl. In a separate bowl, combine the eggs, milk and shortening. Add the liquid mixture to the dry ingredients and stir just enough to barely dampen the flour. Pour the lemon juice over the apples and stir the mix into the batter. Do not over mix. Fill greased muffin tins 2/3 full and bake at 425°F for 25 minutes.

Makes 16 muffins.

APPLE DUMPLINGS

firm green apples
piecrust pastry
sugar
cinnamon, nutmeg and cloves

Peel and core apples, leaving them whole. Roll-out pastry a little thicker than you would for a pie and cut into squares. Set each apple on a large square of pie crust pastry. Fill the center of each apple with sugar and spices and bring pastry up around apple to cover it completely. Place on an ungreased cookie sheet and bake at 350°F for 45 minutes or until golden.

MAPLE BAKED APPLES

crisp apples
maple sugar
chopped walnuts
cinnamon

With a melon-baller, scoop the core out of each apple, taking care not to cut through the very bottom of the blossom end. Stand apples in a baking pan just large enough to hold them all snugly in one layer. Fill the cavities with chopped walnuts and maple sugar or syrup and sprinkle lightly with a pinch of cinnamon. Bake at 350°F until apples are tender. Serve hot or warm with cream or vanilla ice cream.

APPLE BREAD

1/2 c. shortening
1 c. plus 2 tbsp. sugar
1 tbsp. buttermilk
2 eggs, beaten
2 c. flour
1 tsp. baking powder
1 tsp. baking soda
1 tsp. salt
2 c. peeled and finely chopped apples
1 tbsp. grated lemon peel
2/3 c. chopped nuts
1 tsp. vanilla
1 tsp. cinnamon

Cream the shortening and sugar, and beat in the buttermilk and eggs. Sift the baking powder, soda and salt, and add alternately with the apples. Add the remaining ingredients. Pour into a greased loaf pan and bake for 50 to 60 minutes at 350°F.

Storing Apples

Apples keep best and longest if stored between 32°F and 35°F at 80 to 90 percent humidity with moderate air circulation. Under these conditions they should retain flavor, texture and food value, without spoiling, for four to six months. But few homes, even those farmhouses with root cellars, can boast a place that fits that description exactly, from harvest until February. The best most of us can do is come as close to these conditions as we can, check them often and hope for Thanksgiving and Christmas pies.

Cider and Doughnuts

This autumn combination goes together like apple pie and Cheddar cheese—doughnuts must have been invented just to accompany the tangy drink! They are the perfect combination for fall entertaining, whether the cider is sparkling and icy or mulled with whole spices and served piping hot.

Of course, doughnuts are best hot from the kettle. While a cast-iron doughnut kettle on a wood stove lends more atmosphere, an electric skillet makes perfect doughnuts and the temperature is easier to regulate. Have the cooking oil (corn oil produces lighter, healthier doughnuts than the traditional lard) about an inch deep and fry only a few at a time so the oil doesn't cool down too much.

There are many different kinds of doughnuts, but the most successful are made of yeast dough. Let them rise on a cookie sheet covered with waxed paper, from which you can easily slide them into the hot fat. Don't let homemade yeast doughnuts rise too much—their texture should be fairly fine.

© Jerry Howard/Positive Images

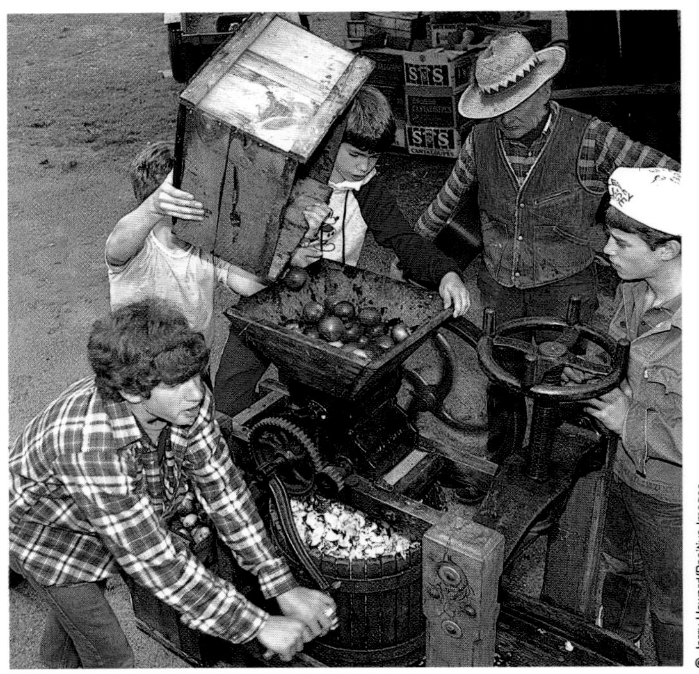

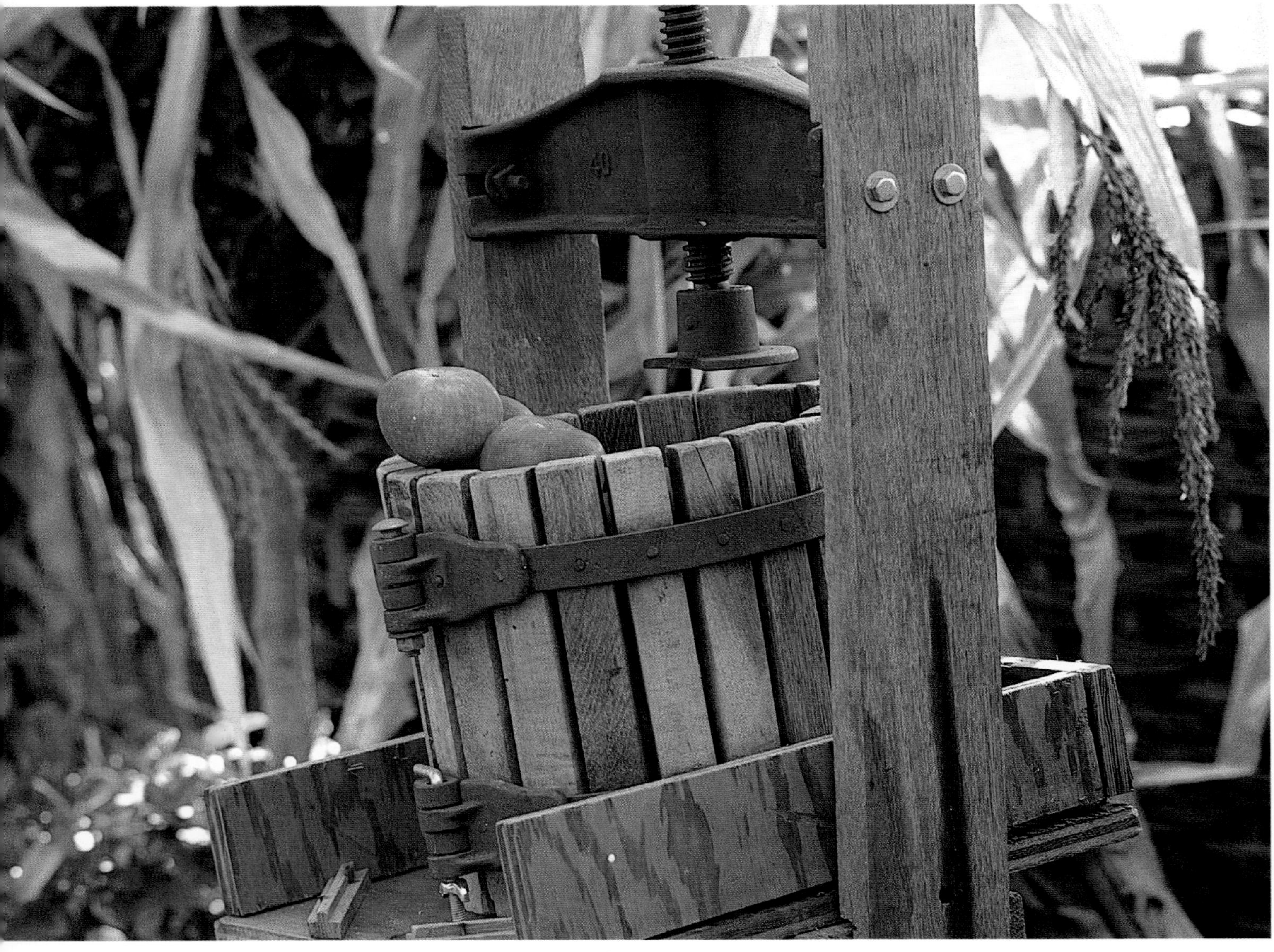

© Anita Sabarese

Doughnuts

1 pkg. yeast
1 c. lukewarm milk
$\frac{1}{2}$ tsp. salt
$3\frac{1}{2}$ c. flour
$\frac{1}{4}$ c. corn oil
1 c. brown sugar
2 eggs, well beaten
$\frac{3}{4}$ tsp. nutmeg

Combine the yeast, milk, salt and $1\frac{1}{2}$ cups of flour in a bowl and beat well. Let rise for $\frac{1}{2}$ hour. Add the remaining ingredients, beat again and allow to rise 1 hour. Punch down and add more flour if the dough seems too soft to roll out. Turn out onto a well-floured board and let dough rest for 10 minutes.

Working with one half of the dough at a time, roll one part $\frac{1}{2}$-inch thick. Cut with a doughnut cutter and let rise, uncovered, for about an hour. Fry at 360°F in corn oil, turning when one side is brown. Remove from the oil with tongs or chopsticks and drain on paper towels. Hot doughnuts may be tossed lightly in a bag of sugar.

Makes approximately 2 dozen doughnuts.

Hot Mulled Cider

2 qts. apple cider
2 cinnamon sticks
1 tsp. whole cloves
1 tsp. whole allspice
orange slices for garnish

In a saucepan, bring the cider, cinnamon sticks, cloves and allspice to a boil and simmer for 10 minutes. Strain piping hot cider into clear glass mugs or pottery cups garnished with long cinnamon sticks and slices of orange.

Makes 2 quarts.

© Robert Perron

Pumpkins

The pumpkin is a fitting symbol for the harvest season. Ripe at this time of year and ready to use, it is also the color of autumn leaves and provides a fine contrast for the black cats, bats and witches of Halloween. Its shape begs to be carved into the leering face of a goblin.

It is also delicious and has culinary uses far beyond the pie. Mashed, it is a good thickener for garden minestrone and makes a splendid cream soup in its own right. Pumpkin bread, pumpkin cookies and even glistening jars of crisp pumpkin pickles and pumpkin marmalade are among the myriad uses for pumpkins.

© Anita Sabarese

© William Seitz

Carving a Jack-o'-Lantern

Cut out the top of a pumpkin, making a hole large enough to accommodate your hand easily. Angle the knife blade slightly toward the center as you cut, or the lid will fall into the pumpkin. Scoop out all the seeds and stringy pulp, leaving a hollow shell. Wash the seeds and spread them out to dry (to make toasted pumpkin seeds, see page 151).

Rotate the pumpkin to find its best "faces." Depending on your self confidence, you can sketch a face first on paper, draw it directly onto the pumpkin with a red marking pen (so you can change your mind without it showing) or cut right in.

When you've finished, set a short candle inside. The jack-o'-lantern will last longer if you remove the lid while the candle is burning. If you put the pumpkin outside, be sure to bring it in when the nights drop below freezing.

© Bob Taylor/FPG International

© Robert Perron

© Ralph B. Pleasant/FPG International

Pumpkin Soup

1 2-lb. pumpkin
2 tbsp. olive oil
2 carrots
1 onion
2 stalks celery
2 c. homemade chicken stock
2 potatoes, cubed
2 tsp. curry powder
1/2 tsp. nutmeg

Peel and seed the pumpkin and cut it into cubes. Chop and sauté carrots, onion and celery in olive oil until soft. Add the chicken stock, potatoes and pumpkin and simmer for 45 minutes. Add seasonings and purée the soup in a blender. Serve hot or cold.

Serves 4.

Pumpkin Pie

piecrust pastry
1 c. packed brown sugar
1 tbsp. flour
1/2 tsp. salt
1 tsp. cinnamon
1/2 tsp. nutmeg
1/2 tsp. cloves
1/2 tsp. ginger
2 c. mashed pumpkin
1 2/3 c. (1 can) evaporated milk
1 egg, slightly beaten

Mix all ingredients in a blender and pour into a 9-inch unbaked pie pastry. Bake at 375°F until filling is set in center, about 50 to 60 minutes.

Pumpkin Marmalade

4 lbs. pumpkin, peeled
4 lbs. sugar
3 lemons
1 orange

Shred the pumpkin and combine with sugar; let stand for 8 hours. Cut the lemons and oranges into very thin slices and add them and any juice to the pumpkin mixture. Simmer until thick and seal in hot jars. Process for 15 minutes.

Makes 6 jars of marmalade.

Pumpkin Pickles

2 1/4 c. sugar
2 1/4 c. vinegar
3 c. water
3 cinnamon sticks
15 cloves
4 lbs. pumpkin

Combine sugar, vinegar, water and spices and boil this syrup for 10 minutes. Peel the pumpkin and cut into 1-inch squares to make about 6 cups. Boil in syrup 5 minutes, then cover and let stand for 1 hour. Then simmer about 1 hour until pumpkin is transparent. Remove spices. Seal in hot jars and process 15 minutes.

Makes 6 jars of pickles.

Toasted Pumpkin Seeds

raw pumpkin seeds
salt

Wash pumpkin seeds well and allow them to almost dry. Place on an ungreased cookie sheet and sprinkle with salt. Toast in a 350°F oven until lightly browned. You can toast these in a broiler, but watch them constantly since they burn quickly. Cool and store in jars.

Hancock Inn Pumpkin Bread

From the Hancock Inn, Hancock, New Hampshire

1 c. brown sugar
1 c. white sugar
1 c. oil
3 eggs
2 to 3 c. mashed pumpkin
1 c. chopped nuts
1 c. raisins
3 c. flour
1/2 tsp. baking powder
1 tsp. baking soda
1/2 tsp. salt
1 1/2 tsp. cloves
1 1/2 tsp. cinnamon
1/2 tsp. allspice
1 1/2 tsp. nutmeg

Mix the sugars and oil. Add the eggs, mashed pumpkin, nuts and raisins. Sift in the flour, baking powder, soda and salt. Stir in the spices. Bake in greased loaf pans at 350°F for 1 to 1 1/2 hours until brown, and done in the middle.

Makes 2 loaves.

© Guy Powers/Envision

The Harvest Soup Pot

Toward late autumn, the garden that was so carefully tended all spring and summer sometimes produces far beyond our expectations. Pickle crocks are full, canning jars are used up, pantry shelves and freezers are close to capacity, but still the vegetables come. Were it not for the soup pot, one would wish for a killing frost!

But the crisp evenings make hearty soups welcome on the menu. This combination of cool weather and late-season plenty is undoubtedly the reason that vegetable soups are a harvest tradition throughout the rural areas of much of the world.

For the gardener, the soup pot is the place for the limp, the lame and the leftover. The outer cabbage leaves that don't make good sauerkraut, the tomatoes that wouldn't fit in the last canning jar, the broccoli stems left after the tender florets went into the freezer.

For purely aesthetic reasons you can cut all the vegetables into fairly uniform-sized pieces. Always add sturdier vegetables first and the greens last.

Garden Chicken Soup

2 tbsp. olive oil
1 onion
3 carrots
5 stalks celery
1 qt. rich chicken broth
1/2 tsp. each, thyme and marjoram
1/2 tsp. curry powder
*rice or small pasta, if desired**
vegetables, such as squash, green beans, peas or shell beans, chopped
salt and pepper to taste
2 c. diced cooked chicken meat
several sprigs of parsley

Chop the onion, carrots, and celery and sauté briefly in the oil in a heavy pot. Add the broth and seasonings and simmer for 1/2 hour. To this basic soup, add chopped vegetables, and simmer until these are cooked. Add chicken meat, garnish with parsley and serve.

*Rice or small pasta may be added—rice 20 minutes before serving and pasta 10 minutes before serving. Either of these will thicken the soup slightly as they cook.

Makes approximately 2 quarts of soup.

Cream of Vegetable Soup

3 tbsp. butter
4 tbsp. flour
2 c. hot chicken broth
2 c. vegetable cooking water
2 c. chopped cooked vegetables (zucchini, celery, broccoli, cauliflower, cucumber, greens, yellow squash or any combination)
1 c. cream
salt and pepper to taste

Melt the butter in a saucepan. Stir in flour and whisk until they are well blended and golden. Add hot broth and stir with whisk until the sauce is smooth. Add the cooking water and stir again. Add vegetables and simmer for 10 minutes. Pour soup into a blender and blend until smooth. Return the mixture to the pan, add cream and salt and pepper to taste. Reheat but do not boil. To freeze this soup leave out the cream and add it at time of serving.

Makes 1 1/2 quarts of soup.

Minestrone

1 ham bone
1/2 c. chopped salt pork or 2 tbsp. olive oil
1 clove garlic
2 onions, chopped
2 carrots, diced
3 stalks celery, chopped
1 c. shell beans
a few leaves each of marjoram, basil, thyme and mint
4 large tomatoes, peeled
1/2 lb. fresh spinach or other greens, chopped
1 c. puréed winter squash or pumpkin
a few sprigs of parsley
salt and pepper, to taste

In a large pot, cover the ham bone with water and simmer for 1 hour. Remove the bone, skim off all fat from the broth. Cut the meat from the bone and set aside. Render salt pork in fry pan (or substitute 2 tablespoons of olive oil for the salt pork) and sauté the garlic, onion, carrot and celery without browning. Add the sautéed vegetables, beans, herbs and tomatoes to the broth. Simmer until the beans are tender. Add the greens and squash and let simmer for another 30 minutes. Season to taste with salt and pepper.

If you do not have shell beans, substitute dried beans that have been soaked and partially cooked first. Lentils and chickpeas are a good addition, as well. Nearly any vegetable can be added to this basic recipe.

Makes approximately 2 quarts of soup.

© Stanley Joseph

Winter Fun

For all the biting winds and the chilly toes and noses it brings, winter has its special charms. Thousands flock north each year to enjoy the ski slopes, frozen ponds and woodland trails winter creates. Winter is a special time to be in the country.

© William Seitz

North Wind Picture Archives

North Wind Picture Archives

Cross-Country Skiing

Unlike downhill skiing, cross-country skiing involves little investment. Equipment is not expensive, trail fees are minimal—you can even ski free in your backyard or through the woods. You can go with a group in a spirited skiing party that ends in front of a fireplace, or alone to listen to the sparkling silence of the winter woods.

Cross-country skiing is a sport for all ages; it can be as strenuous or as relaxed as you choose. No special clothing is required, but several light layers which can be shed are better than a heavy coat. While there are elegant cross-country ski outfits, blue jeans over long underwear with a sweater and light windbreaker is the most popular "uniform" for country people skiing through the woods.

© William Seitz

© Rogers Associates

Sugaring-Off Party

Tapping maple trees and boiling the clear sap until it is a rich amber-colored syrup is a country tradition wherever sugar maples grow in the United States and Canada. Syrup making was one of many skills the Native Americans taught the early settlers, and the techniques have changed remarkably little to this day. Plastic tubes connecting the trees to large vats may have replaced traditional equipment on commercial sugar bushes, as maple groves are called, but old buckets hanging from stately maples are still a common sight in March. And the traditional sugaring-off party hasn't changed a bit.

People gather at sugaring-off parties for fun, work and camaraderie. But mostly they're there for the first taste of maple syrup. A good way to try it is to make "leather aprons." This is done by heating the syrup to 242 degrees, and then drizzling it onto a plate full of fresh, clean, untrampled snow. It will harden to a chewy candy which you can wind onto a fork and eat. The traditional accompaniments for this sticky treat are fresh unsweetened doughnuts and sour pickles.

North Wind Picture Archives

Building a Snowman

Building a snowman has always been a favorite wintertime activity for both young and old. A snowman can be built in any style, detailed or plain, but it is always made entirely of snow rolled into great balls and stacked one upon the other.

Building a snowman requires the right kind of snow—the sticky stuff that is more common toward the beginning and end of winter when the weather is a little warmer; the kind that covers the landscape quickly and sticks to every twig. Only this kind of snow is sticky enough for a small ball to be rolled across a lawn and grow as it rolls until it is too big to push any farther.

Lift a smaller ball up onto the first (or roll it up a slanted board if it is too heavy), and top it with an even smaller head. Pack handfuls of snow around the snowballs to hold them together. You can sculpt the balls into any shape you want. Then, finish off with a hat, a scarf, a carrot nose, coal or button eyes, and give it a broom to hold, although a snow shovel might seem more appropriate.

© Lynn Karlin

A Backyard Skating Rink

Some backyards—those with a natural dip or depression—form skating rinks with little or no help. Once the ground freezes thoroughly it takes only a good dose of water from the garden hose to form a rink that lasts until the spring thaw.

But if your land doesn't have a natural sink, if the soil is particularly sandy, or if there are frequent thaws, nature will need the help of some large beams and sheet plastic.

Choose the lowest and most level spot available and remove all stones and sharp weed stems. After the ground is thoroughly frozen, outline the rink with heavy beams or railway ties.

Spread a sheet of heavy, clear plastic (don't use black, which will absorb heat from the sun and melt your rink) over the rink and beams. One side at a time, tuck the plastic under the outer edge of the beams so that it covers the beams completely and is well anchored from the wind. This forms a shallow, plastic bowl. Don't walk on the plastic since it is quite brittle when cold.

Use a garden hose to flood the plastic base. Be sure to empty and take the hose inside after each use so it won't freeze and burst. It is best to freeze the rink in several stages. If large air bubbles form under the plastic as you flood, pull the edges of the plastic to disperse these before the water freezes.

For smooth skating, shovel it as soon after a new snowfall as possible, sweep it and give it a light spray of water to protect the surface. Sweep and spray the ice every once in a while even if it doesn't snow.

© Holt Confer/Image Works

Sleigh Ride!

The magic of a sleigh ride through the winter night behind a team of horses, sleigh bells jingling, is one of winter's greatest pleasures. Snuggling under lap robes, the wind stinging cheeks and noses, puts everyone in a good mood. Someone starts a favorite song or a well-loved carol and soon a blend of voices rings out across the frozen fields. The best sleigh rides occur under a full moon. Invariably the sleigh ride ends at a warm, glowing fireside with hot mulled wine, cider or steaming cocoa (see recipes, page 165) all around.

For the lucky few who are in or near Manchester, Vermont, after Christmas, the sleigh ride ends at the grand doorway of Hildene. This country estate,

North Wind Picture Archives

on the crest of a hill overlooking the Green Mountains, was built by Abraham Lincoln's son. It is open to daytime visitors year-round, but only on these few special sleigh ride evenings is it open at night.

The sleigh ride begins at the foot of the hill. From there, the guests are drawn by teams of huge draft horses, through the woods and up to the house, each window invitingly lit by a candle. Hildene's rooms are bright with holiday decorations from the woods and fields that surround it, and music from a pipe organ welcomes the arriving guests. While any sleigh ride is a special treat, one which ends at a period country house ablaze with Christmas hospitality is an unforgettable experience.

North Wind Picture Archives

Sledding

The appeal of sleds, from sleek bobsleds to makeshift sheets of cardboard, is almost universal. Find a hill covered with snow and there's a good chance it will be criss-crossed with sled-tracks. Toboggans, traverse sleds, and flying saucers are only a few of the many forms sleds have taken through the centuries, as adults and children alike have sought the thrill of flying down an icy slope at top speed.

In some towns in Switzerland, where sleighs and skis are still everyday transportation, the streets are not sanded. It is a common sight in towns like Lenk to see toddlers, all bundled up on their stroller sleds, being pulled by busy mothers.

Some towns in New England and other northern areas set aside hills or even streets for community sledding, and anyone with a sloping backyard can enjoy the sport at home. While most sleds are interchangeable, certain styles work better in different conditions. Sleds with runners slide best on ice or packed snow, while flat-bottomed sleds such as flying saucers or toboggans slide better on loose snow.

Invite friends of all ages to a sledding party and follow it with hot chocolate or mulled cider in front of the fireplace—and know that you are joining in a winter tradition enjoyed wherever there are snow and hills.

HOT SPICED COCOA

Nothing warms the hands and the heart on an icy day quite like a steaming mug of hot cocoa. Although we think of it as a drink of the frosty climates, not the tropics, the Aztecs of Mexico introduced hot cocoa to the world. Mexicans still serve it in country inns in the mountains, rich and dark and spicy, whipped to a froth with a special wooden whisk rolled between the palms of the hands.

1 c. milk
2 cinnamon sticks
4 whole cloves
2 heaping tbsp. dark powdered cocoa
3 rounded tbsp. superfine sugar

Bring the milk, a broken cinnamon stick and 4 whole cloves just to the boil. Place the cocoa and the sugar into a cup. Strain enough of the milk into the cup to moisten the cocoa and sugar, and stir well. Add the rest of the hot milk. Whisk to a froth with a wooden cocoa stirrer or a small wire whisk. Serve with a long cinnamon stick.

Makes 1 serving.

HOT MULLED WINE

1 cinnamon stick
4 whole cloves
1 slice lemon
1/2 c. sherry
1 bottle red wine
sugar to taste

Place the spices and lemon peel in a large saucepan, cover with water, and simmer for 15 minutes. Strain, and add the sherry, wine and sugar. Heat but do not boil.

Makes 6 servings.

A Winter Tea

Teatime is said to have originated in the great private country estates of England as a diversion to keep guests occupied in the period between the afternoon's activities and the dinner hour. A custom still practiced in England, it is also observed by many country inns in America. Teatime offers a quiet break during the day to relax and meet fellow guests.

You can achieve that same unhurried hospitality in your home. Your respite from the day's activities can be as elegant or as simple as you choose. It will revolve, of course, around a steaming pot of rich, fresh-brewed tea. Darjeeling and Assam are good choices. If you are entertaining a large group, you may wish to prepare several different teas. This is a fine way to show off and use a collection of china teapots.

The centerpiece should be a bowl or basket of fresh greens. Tea napkins can be made for the occasion from one of the print calicos available from fabric stores; the tablecloth should be a solid color to offset the assortment of goodies covering it.

Three fine country inns that serve particularly elegant teas share their favorite recipes here:

Shortbread Fingers

From The Orchards, Williamstown, Massachusetts.

$1\frac{1}{4}$ c. plus 2 tbsp. butter, slightly softened
$\frac{3}{4}$ c. sugar
$\frac{1}{4}$ tsp. salt
$3\frac{1}{3}$ c. flour

Cream the softened butter, sugar and salt, and beat until fluffy. Gently work the flour into the mixture. Wrap dough in plastic and refrigerate for 30 minutes.

Prepare a greased baking sheet and preheat the oven to 375°F. Using a lightly floured surface, roll out the dough to fit baking sheet; trim dough if necessary. With a fork, pierce the shortbread in several places. Bake about 30 minutes until golden brown.

Cut warm shortbread into strips and sprinkle generously with sugar. Cool on baking sheet, then transfer the shortbread to a rack until completely cooled.

Makes about 48 fingers.

Jarlsberg Mini Scones

From The King's Cottage, Lancaster, Pennsylvania.

2 c. sifted all-purpose flour
2 tbsp. sugar
1 tbsp. baking powder
$\frac{1}{2}$ tsp. salt
$\frac{1}{4}$ c. butter
$\frac{1}{2}$ c. grated Jarlsberg cheese
3 tbsp. currants
2 eggs
$\frac{1}{2}$ c. milk

Combine dry ingredients and cut in butter until mixture resembles coarse crumbs. Add cheese and currants.

In another bowl, beat the eggs until light; add milk. Gradually stir into flour mixture. Roll out on lightly floured board to $\frac{1}{2}$-inch thickness. Cut into 2-inch squares; cut each in half on the diagonal to form triangles. Brush each top with milk. Place on greased baking sheet and bake at 375°F for 20 minutes or until golden brown. Serve warm.

Makes about 30 scones.

Cottage Cookies

From The King's Cottage, Lancaster, Pennsylvania.

$\frac{1}{2}$ c. sugar
$\frac{1}{2}$ c. butter
2 egg yolks
1 tsp. vanilla
$1\frac{1}{2}$ c. sifted flour
1 tsp. baking powder
$\frac{1}{2}$ tsp. salt

Topping:
2 egg whites
1 c. brown sugar

Cream butter and sugar; add egg yolks and stir. Mix in the remaining batter ingredients and stir until mixed well. Spread the batter in an ungreased 8-by-8-inch pan.

For the topping, beat the egg whites until stiff and add brown sugar (you can add a cup of chopped nuts to this if you like). Pour the topping over the dough in the pan. Bake at 325° F for 45 minutes. Allow to cool and cut into bars.

Makes about 2 dozen cookies.

Maple Scones

From the Inn of the Six Mountains, Killington, Vermont.

1 1/4 c. all-purpose flour
2 1/4 tsp. double-acting baking powder
1/2 tsp. salt
1/4 c. sweet butter, chilled
2 eggs, beaten
1/4 c. heavy cream
3 tbsp. maple syrup
1/3 c. chopped pecans or walnuts
2 tbsp. brown sugar

Maple Glaze:
3/4 c. sifted confectioners' sugar
1/4 c. pure maple syrup

Combine flour, baking powder and salt. Cut in chilled butter until it is the consistency of cornmeal. Set aside 2 tablespoons of the beaten egg. In a separate bowl, combine the remaining egg, cream and maple syrup. Make a well in the dry ingredients and add the egg mixture all at once. Combine with as few strokes as possible.

Handling the dough gently, place on a gently floured board and roll to 3/4-inch thickness. With a cookie cutter, cut into 4-inch rounds and cut each round into 6 triangles. Place on a cookie sheet and brush with the remaining egg. Bake at 450°F until delicately browned, about 10 to 15 minutes.

While the scones are baking, make the maple glaze. Stir together the confectioners' sugar and maple syrup until well mixed. Drizzle over scones after they have cooled.

Makes 2 dozen scones.

Tea Napkins

One-half yard of calico fabric, 45 inches wide will make ten tea-sized napkins. Measuring carefully, cut the fabric into 9-inch squares, removing both selvedges. Be sure edges are cut straight. With the point of a large needle, separate a few threads from one edge and ravel them out, continuing until you have a fringe about 1/4-inch wide. Repeat on each side.

Eyelet Napkin Rings

Cut strips of double-edged white insertion eyelet into 5-inch lengths. With right sides facing, stitch the cut ends together to form loops. Turn right side out and run narrow red or green ribbon through the insertion space, tying the ends in bows. To use, fold napkin in fourths and roll it into a tube. Slide on the eyelet ring and adjust the napkin so it is even.

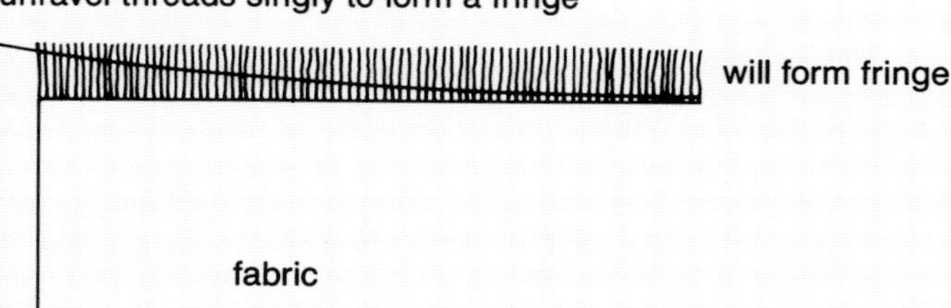

C · H · A · P · T · E · R

6

Christmas in the Country

Christmas has become almost as much a celebration of a season as a religious holiday. And nowhere is this more true than in the country. Celebrations in the country are a time of sleigh rides, snowmen and big family get togethers.

Like the holiday itself, the Christmas decorating theme doesn't have to be religious. The greens and reds of Christmas are universally appealing. And you'll find that their appeal won't wear off after the holiday passes.

You don't have to live in the woods to decorate your house in the country-Christmas style. But if you do live in the country, you're lucky.

Christmas is an especially exciting time of year in the country, where the herbs, greens and flowers that play such a role in the lore of the season are readily available. Fresh greens—whether needled conifers or broadleaf evergreens—can form the basis for decorating. And wild berries—red alder, bright bittersweet, rosehips and others—along with dried herbs and everlasting flowers provide bright color accents.

Nothing says Christmas more than a colorful tree. These handcrafted wooden ornaments, shiny balls and candy canes are perfect country Christmas decorations. And everyone loves stringing popcorn for the tree.

Decking the Halls

Swags, long bunches of herbs and dried flowers carefully arranged and tied with a bow, are lovely to hang in narrow areas between doors and windows or over doorways, where a wreath would be too big. Door facings, corner posts, beams, corners and even doors themselves are perfect places to put swags.

Swags require some long-stemmed and fairly full plant material—Silver King artemisia is a good base, as are branches of bay or rosemary. Fresh greens also work well, especially fragrant ones such as balsam or cedar.

Lay a long spray of this base material on a flat work surface. Add dried flowers with stems, the spike shapes first to fan out as a background, then those with clusters of flowers. Balance the arrangement for both color and density. Anchor each addition by wiring it to the main stem of the background spray, covering these stems with more plant material as you work down. The stems at the base can be covered with short sprigs of full-foliaged material, such as sage, lamb's ears or bay. Tie a neat bow of wide ribbon around the lower stems and cover the ends below the bow by pushing short foliage upward into the bow from the bottom.

© Stephen McBrady/PhotoEdit

The Christmas Mantel

The hearth and mantel, along with the Christmas tree, become the focal point of a room at Christmas time. Hang stockings from the mantel (you can install permanent hooks in the underside of the mantel shelf where they won't show). The shelf itself can become a winter village, hold a fan-shaped arrangement of winter greens or be decorated with *scherrenschnitte,* a Pennsylvania Dutch paper-cut border.

Of course you must keep the hearth free of decoration if you use the fireplace. But if you don't use it, spread a sheet in it and fill the fireplace with large wrapped gifts, arranged as though they were tumbling out. A collection of baskets can fill the fireplace or it can simply be set for a fire with white birch logs in the andirons.

The overmantel wall is a good place for a large wreath, especially one fashioned of dried flowers and herbs.

Tabletop Trees

Small trees with full foliage that can be used for centerpieces are difficult to find, but you can make them from branches of evergreen or even some herb plants, such as rosemary, bay or boxwood. Begin with a cone of absorbent floral arranging foam and cover it with chicken wire for strength. Insert branches, each sloping down slightly, beginning at the bottom of the cone. Use very short sprigs toward the top, since the cone is smaller there. At the very top, use a spire-shaped sprig or simply insert a sharp stick upon which you can put a multisided star or other decoration. Decorate these trees with strawflowers or other dried flowers. Be sure to keep plenty of water in a plate under the base so the foam will stay moist.

Small, natural tabletop trees about three feet tall can be decorated for display on kitchen countertops and hall tables, though they are too tall for dining table use. Since they are small, they are best adorned with a theme in mind, such as gingerbread, or with one type of ornament so they don't look overdone.

An entire tree can be decorated with small pretzels, red satin bows tied to the bottom of each. The pretzel loop can be pushed onto the tip of a branch quite easily. Small decorated cookies or gingerbread figures can be pierced while still hot from the oven with a hole at the top for hanging them on small trees. Look around for other small items that are light and easy to hang in small places, such as miniature candy canes.

Country Ornaments to Make

Part of the fun of decorating a Christmas tree is creating the ornaments. There are many choices. An entire tree can be decorated with ornaments made from the gifts of nature: cones, seedpods, milkweed, corn husks, nuts, dried flowers. Collect calico fabric in tiny red and green prints and an assortment of laces, trims and ribbons for another theme.

A trip to the craft supply store will yield a great stock of precut wooden shapes, basket cane, and other items that can be painted, decorated and combined in a number of ways. Don't worry if painting is not your specialty; some of the most charming of these simply involve staining or painting a solid color and gluing them together. Tiny wooden hearts can be painted red and glued to wreaths made by winding basket cane around a glass and tying it with ribbon. Hearts can also be glued to wooden teddies covered with brown wood stain, and finished off with a red bow around the teddy's neck. Half the fun is thinking up new combinations of materials.

Wrap wooden sheep shapes in raw wool or natural-color yarn after painting the feet and nose black. Decorate miniature slates in a variety of ways, writing a special Christmas message with a tailor's marker. An entire tree can be covered with these whimsical wooden ornaments.

Tiny oval and round wooden boxes painted in country colors or left natural and stenciled with tiny designs such as strawberries or apples make excellent gifts as well as charming decorations. Make hangers by closing a ribbon loop in the lid, or stack a set of three boxes and tie with embroidery thread in a contrasting color. Glue tiny country pictures to the lids and edging with narrow picot lace or narrow ribbon.

Milkweed pods make perfect frames for miniature dried flower arrangements, and pinecones can be made into a variety of ornaments. Walnut shells can be painted red and capped with green felt hulls to create strawberries.

A whole collection of country mice is easy to make from oven-fired clay, which comes in a variety of colors. Imbed a hairpin in each as a hanger before baking. These mice can hold gifts, teddy bears, musical instruments, trees or other small objects.

Woolly Lambs

White fleece fabric looks a lot like lamb's wool, and you can combine it with black felt, white glue and clothespins to make adorable lamb decorations for the Christmas tree.

Cut ovals from the fleece about 3 inches long and 2½ inches wide. You will need two for each lamb. Also cut four strips of black felt ¼-by-1 inch long and a piece about 1-by-½ inch, rounded at one end to look like a nose. A tiny thin snip makes a tail.

Lay one fleece oval fuzzy side down and arrange the black felt to form the head, feet (which can be set at angles to give the appearance of a sheep running) and a tail. Attach these with tiny drops of glue. Put another drop of glue on the other side of each of the felt pieces to attach them to the second oval. Place it, fleece up, over the first. Hold together at glue points with clip clothespins until the glue is dry. Add a hanger of yarn or invisible thread.

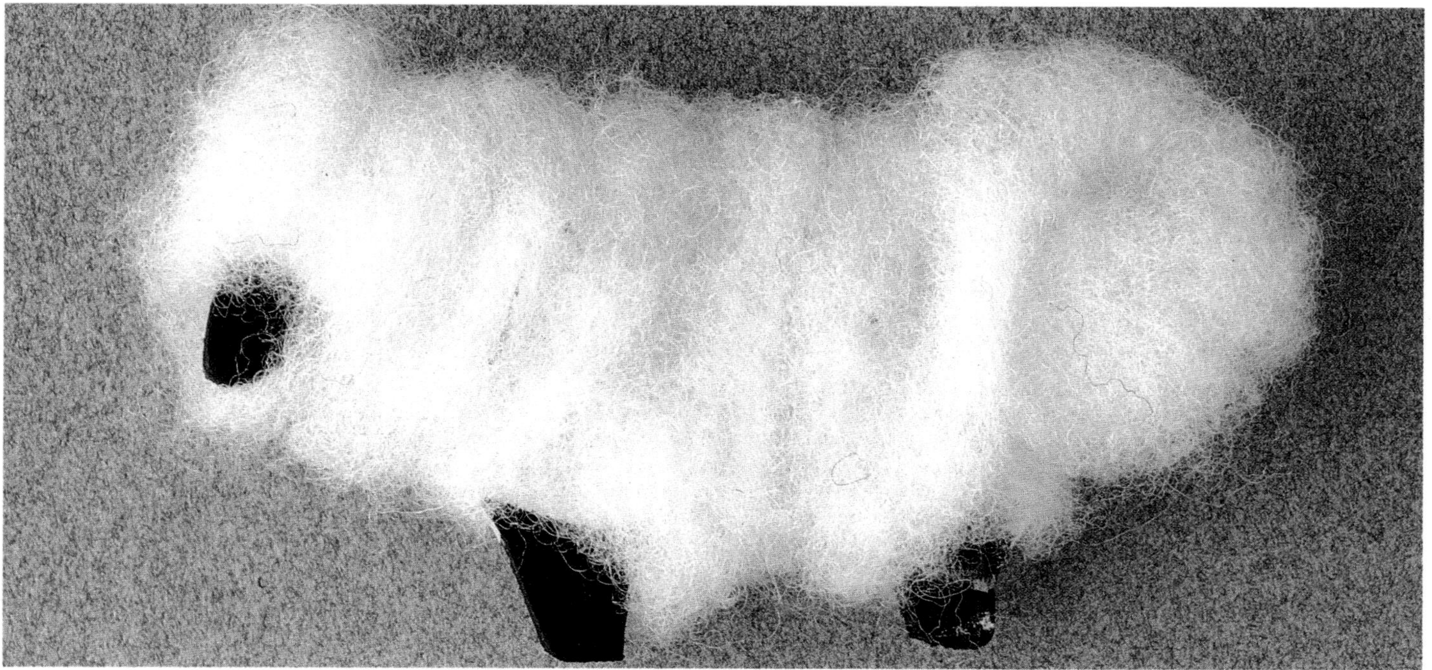

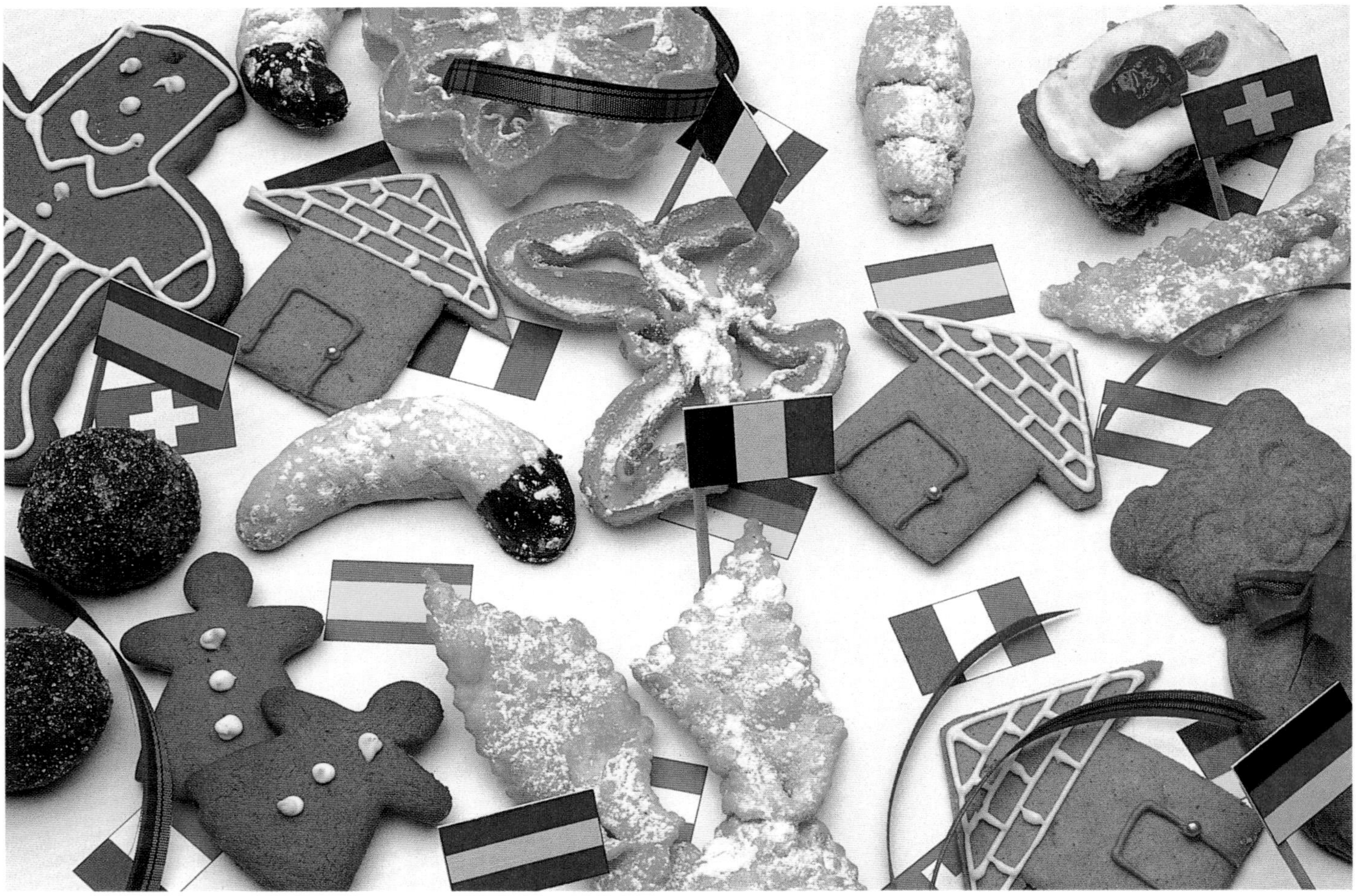

© John Pemberton

Cookie Party

Baking and decorating Christmas sugar cookies is a treasured tradition in many families, and for many, a good occasion for inviting friends to join in. Ahead of time, bake trays of sugar cookies cut in fancy shapes and prepare several batches of frosting in a variety of holiday colors. Assemble colored sugars, silver shot, jimmies and other decorations.

Make pastry bags from sheets of bakers' parchment and fit them with fancy decorating tips. Spread everything out on a big kitchen table, or several card tables, and have a pot of tea ready for guests when they arrive. A full teapot is important because cookies are bound to break under the strain of the frosting, and your guests will want to wash them down with tea.

There are no rules. Everyone's creative talents can shine through. Be prepared, with extra white frosting that can be colored when needed. Be sure to have plenty of space to spread frosted cookies out until the frosting hardens, and a supply of pizza boxes so favorite cookies can be carried home safely in a single layer.

Of course, you don't have to invite people in to decorate cookies. A family party where everyone, even small children, has free rein to decorate cookies, could become an annual tradition.

© Vincent Serbin/Leo deWys Inc.

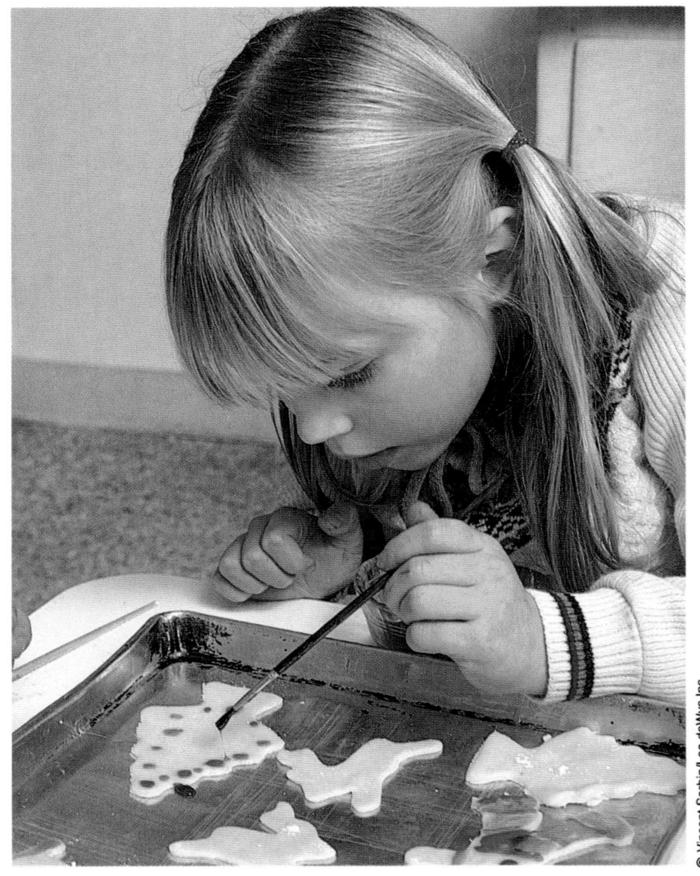

Gingerbread People

Gingerbread people are a good project for children since the dough is not sticky or difficult to handle. Gingerbread cutters are available in all sizes, from 1-inch tall to over-sized German designs.

1/4 c. molasses
1/4 c. sugar
3 tbsp. butter or shortening
1 tbsp. milk
2 c. flour
1/2 tsp. baking soda
1/2 tsp. salt
1 tsp. ginger
1/2 tsp. cloves
1/2 tsp. cinnamon
raisins and currants for decoration

In a small saucepan, heat molasses just to boiling and add the sugar, butter and milk. In a bowl, sift dry ingredients together and stir them into the molasses mixture, adding more flour, if necessary, to make the dough stiff enough to roll. Using one small piece of dough at a time, roll to just under 1/4-inch thick and cut out the gingerbread people. To decorate before baking, use currants or raisins for faces and buttons.

Bake at 375°F until the cookies begin to darken on the bottom. It may help to keep the unused dough in the refrigerator while each batch is being rolled out.

Yield depends upon how big your cookie cutters are.

Gingerbread For Modeling

For those who enjoy modeling with clay, here is a gingerbread dough that works easily and holds its shape when baked. Santa faces with mustaches and thick beards, even woolly sheep (make the wool by pressing dough through a garlic press), and gnomes with tall pointed hats can be created with this dough.

2 c. flour
1 tsp. ground ginger
1/2 tsp. baking soda
1/4 tsp. salt
1/2 tsp. cinnamon
1/2 c. molasses
4 tbsp. sugar
2 tbsp. oil
2 tbsp. milk

Sift dry ingredients together. In a large bowl, mix remaining ingredients and sift the dry mixture into these, mixing well. Work dough with your hands, adding a bit more flour or milk to make it the consistency of modeling clay. Bake as for gingerbread people.

Sugar Cookies

1/2 c. butter
3/4 c. sugar
1 egg
1/2 tsp. vanilla
1 tbsp. milk
1 1/4 c. flour
1/4 tsp. salt
1/4 tsp. baking powder

Cream butter and sugar until light. Beat in the egg and vanilla, add milk and beat again. Sift the dry ingredients together and stir them into the liquid mixture to make a smooth dough. Chill well (until dough is cold) and roll out on a floured board. Cut into shapes and bake cookies at 375°F until lightly browned. Cool on racks.

Makes approximately 20 5-by-3 1/2-inch cookies.

Cookie Frosting

1/4 c. butter
1/4 c. milk
confectioners' sugar

In a saucepan, melt the butter and add milk. Beat in enough confectioners' sugar to make a stiff frosting that will hold its shape when spread. Tint with a few drops of food coloring. Store this in covered containers in the refrigerator until ready to use.

PLEASANT STREET
INN

C · H · A · P · T · E · R 7

Country Traveling

Weary of the sameness of chain hotels, North Americans recently have begun to discover the charm of staying at country inns. European travelers have long favored the personal, relaxed hospitality of the inns. Now demand for homey hotels has led to their proliferation throughout the United States and Canada.

Inns differ, not only from hotels and motels, but from each other, in style, size, services and facilities. But all of them have atmosphere in common. They are relaxed, hospitable, personal and friendly. Staying in one is much like being a weekend guest at an English country estate. Hosts are congenial, helpful, and they enjoy people.

The smallest of these inns are often known as bed and breakfasts (B&Bs), since breakfast is always included. The owners have converted some portion of their private homes into guest rooms. Very often these are historic homes and great care and attention has been given to their restoration.

This grand Victorian home is really a small, quiet hotel, appropriately named The Pleasant Street Inn. Situated on a hill above the Harbor in Rockport, Massachusetts, this inn is typical of the warm hotels available to country travelers. All the guest rooms have been carefully restored, and one even has a spiral staircase leading to its own private tower.

Relax for a While

Country inns offer more rooms than B&Bs and are not private homes, although they share much of the ambiance of B&Bs. Very often set in historic taverns or plantations, these have a gentle, unhurried air and personal warmth not found in hotels.

Instead of a lobby with a reception desk, guests usually enter a foyer. There are often dining rooms where guests can have dinner, and parlours, gardens and verandas where guests can relax. While they welcome the traveler who is just passing through, these are places you could settle in to spend a few days.

Larger than either of these and combining the best qualities of inns with the special luxuries and activities of a resort are the larger inns and country resort hotels. These are often fine old resorts in mountain or shore settings, but many include modern luxuries without sacrificing the warmth, hospitality and special flavor of an old-fashioned inn.

Each of the country inns in the gallery that follows is outstanding both for its style and hospitality, and each is in a region rich in attractions for the country traveler.

Kent Manor Inn, Kent Island, Maryland.

© Rogers Associates

A Gallery of Country Inns

THE KING'S COTTAGE, in a quiet neighborhood of Lancaster, Pennsylvania, is an elegant, beautifully restored Spanish-style mansion offering skillfully decorated guest rooms.

Antiques, deep carpets, stained glass and well chosen accessories fill the house. Guests are greeted with tea served in the library and welcomed home in the evening with cordials and chocolates by the fire. Breakfast here is what guests remember most—fresh fruit compote of melon, kiwi and berries, French toast topped with butter into which peaches have been whipped, fresh Lancaster County sausage and pure maple syrup.

Lancaster is in the middle of one of the finest areas for country travelers, with many Amish farms, craft shows and shops, entire towns devoted to antiques, quilt shows, farmers markets, auctions and rural festivals.

THE PLEASANT STREET INN in Rockport, Massachusetts, is a grand Victorian home complete with cupola, set on a quiet hilltop high above the harbor. Its rich oak woodwork and polished floors have been restored and each room is carefully furnished with comfortable beds, deep chairs and decorative touches that include fresh flowers. Unique architectural features make the inn especially charming; one room has a spiral staircase leading to its own private reading nook in the tower; and most of the rooms have either window seats, bay windows or both.

The Rockport-Cape Anne area offers harbor cruises, whale watching, clambakes, antique shops galore and all the attractions of the New England coast.

THE CRYSTAL RIVER INN, in San Marcos, Texas, is a warm old Texas inn, with tall columns in the Greek revival style. There are eight guest rooms, each named after a central Texas river. Some have canopied beds and fireplaces. Breakfast is a big meal at the Crystal River Inn, with Texas Eggs Benedict, made with cornbread and brandied white sauce, and other treats. The owners can arrange for you to go white-water rafting, ballooning or swimming. You can even go for a llama ride in the nearby hills.

THE OBAN INN is a classically Canadian place that is mix of old world England and the new world. And it's a lovely place to stay all year round—even in the winter, when snow covers everything. The inn is located in the historic village of Niagara-on-the-Lake, Ontario, near Toronto, and just across the river from Fort Niagara, in the United States. The Oban Inn is a wonderful place for English country meals, such as Yorkshire pudding and roast beef. You can join the other guests in singing around the piano if you like.

THE PATCHWORK QUILT COUNTRY INN, in Middlebury, Indiana, is actually a working farm in the heart of farm country. There are only three guest rooms here, so you won't be overwhelmed by the other guests. The inn is famous for its evening buffet, which might include roast beef, ham, fried chicken and enough side dishes to fill your plate. Staying here would be a great way to discover the true Midwestern country style.

THE HANDFIELD INN (Auberge Handfield) is the place to go if you like French food, French customs and listening to French. Visiting this Inn in St. Marc-sur-le-Richelieu, Quebec is like visiting a small town in France. The rooms are decorated in the old Quebec style, with antiques and finely crafted furniture. The Inn is on the bank of the Richelieu river, so you can pass an afternoon watching the small boats sail by. From the first week of March to the end of April there are sugaring-off parties, where maple tree sap is boiled down to make maple syrup.

KENT MANOR INN is on Kent Island, near Annapolis, Maryland. This farmhouse was converted into a stately mansion many years ago when a wing was added. Its current owner has restored the original home and altered the wing to match it down to the last detail. Its wide verandas overlook fields and the Chesapeake Bay. Each of the twenty-five guest rooms is individually furnished—when the owner could not find original sleigh beds for several rooms, he had them custom built. The restaurant here brings the finishing touch to a fine inn, with an inspired menu and carefully prepared dishes.

THE JASPER PARK LODGE in Jasper, Alberta, Canada is a full-service luxury resort, set between the Rocky Mountains and a lake, and standing amid tall pines. But its atmosphere is distinctly that of a wealthy family's rustic hunting lodge. The area surrounding the inn has a wealth of wildlife.

The entrance is guarded by totem poles and the lobby is dominated by a huge stone fireplace. Guest rooms are found in the main lodge, cedar chalets and log cabins. The inn's dining rooms specialize in wild game dishes, just as one would expect from a mountain lodge.

FOOTHILL HOUSE in Calistoga, California, offers a different style of country accommodation in a simple turn-of-the-century farmhouse. Nestled among trees that provide cooling shade in summer, the inn offers both mountain scenery and local wildlife. The color scheme for each room is determined by the handmade quilt on the four-poster bed, and each room has a working fireplace. Breakfast is served in the sun room, on the terrace or in guests' rooms, and local wines and cheese are served in the afternoon.

RANCHO CAYMUS INN in Rutheford, California, is a living showplace for the artists who created and furnished it. Built in the Spanish style, its suites surround a garden that is both rustic and luxurious. The interior is entirely handmade—solid oak doors, hewn beams of California black walnut, handcrafted pottery basins, carved walnut beds, wrought-iron lamps, Parota wood furniture carved in Guadalajara, Mexico, and rugs, bedspreads and tapestries dyed and woven by South American Indians. The inn is a living folk art museum.

The Napa Valley area offers wine festivals as well as vineyard tours and tastings at over 100 wineries. The valley is rich in scenery and offers outdoor sports for the more active.

ABIGAIL'S, on Vancouver Island in British Columbia, is one of the most elegant bed and breakfast inns in Canada. The large library has leather furniture, antique rugs, polished hardwood floors and granite fireplaces. All of the 16 rooms are filled with antiques, and some have fireplaces. A full breakfast is served. Vancouver Island is a charming place, with tea rooms, seashore, forests and beautiful gardens. You get there by ferry from Washington state or Vancouver.

THE OLD RITTENHOUSE INN, in Bayfield, Wisconsin, is a Victorian home that has been decorated with lovely antiques collected by the owners. Close to Madeline Island, in Lake Superior, the inn is in an area that offers a lot of outdoor activities, including snow skiing, hiking, and an apple festival in the fall. The inn offers "mystery weekends" year-round. The dining room serves fresh lake trout, homemade bread and other delights. There's even a little shop where you can buy the homemade preserves, candy and fruit you eat in the dining room.

The sunporch at King's Cottage, Lancaster, Pennsylvania (opposite page); The Orchards, Williamstown, Massachusetts.

Courtesy The Orchards/© Randy O'Rourke

THE ORCHARDS, an English-style country house in Williamstown, Massachusetts, is thought by many to be the finest inn in New England. Bay windows, fine antiques, down pillows and a private bakeshop characterize this getaway. A specialty is afternoon tea, complete with scones and cream, tea sandwiches and delicacies from the bakeshop. Tea is served from one of the sixty-one sterling silver pots in The Orchards' collection.

The surrounding Berkshire mountains offer the nation's foremost outdoor music festival, theater, skiing, hiking, historic towns and classic New England scenery.

Courtesy White Swan Tavern

White Swan Tavern, Chestertown, Maryland (above); The Jared Coffin House, Nantucket Island, Massachusetts.

WHITE SWAN TAVERN in Chestertown, Maryland, is right out of the Revolutionary era, each room filled with antiques from the period in which the room was added to the original tavern. One suite is in late Victorian, another has a netted canopy bed and the old kitchen on the first floor (the only guest room with handicapped access) has been converted into a unique and charming room with a gigantic fireplace and handwoven coverlets.

Chestertown was once Maryland's most important seaport, and its streets lined with restored homes are great for strolling. Nearby Mount Harmon Plantation offers the flavor of another era and style of country living, with views of the tidal rivers and vast rolling fields.

GRINKLE PARK in northern Yorkshire, England, is approached on a drive lined with lush green rhododendrons covered with giant pink blossoms in the spring, that opens suddenly to reveal the graceful stone Victorian manor house. Inside is a pure English country house; huge wing chairs welcome the weary traveler and a tea tray is brought to the fireside table.

Guest rooms are named for the birds and flowers found on neighboring moors, and each is decorated in a style of its own, with art, antiques, draperies and even bed linens chosen to complement the style.

In summer, tea is served on the lawn or in the camellia-filled conservatory overlooking the lawns, pond, woodland and fields. The menu at Grinkle Park includes many wild game specialties from the estate and breakfast is the inn's own sausages and smoked fish.

The surrounding countryside, boasting a fine museum of country life, is just as pleasant as the inn itself.

THE COMPASS ROSE, on Grand Manan Island, New Brunswick, Canada is exactly what you would expect a turn-of-the-century seaside guest house to be. Country warmth and hospitality—nothing "cute" or trendy—is the style here. Rooms are furnished with old pine furniture, hooked rugs and patterned wallpapers, perfect for the neat cottages overlooking the fishing harbor of North Head. Fresh vegetables from the Compass Rose's own garden, local seafood and wild fruits and berries found on the island are on the dinner menu.

Staying here is like being a guest in someone's home, with comfortable chairs in front of the fireplace, the teakettle always hot in the kitchen, and shared baths. This is not a luxury inn, but the pampering here is in a class by itself, and Grand Manan is a paradise for the bird watcher, nature lover, photographer or artist—or anyone else who wants to relax on a quiet island.

THE TIDEWATER INN in Easton, Maryland, is perhaps the best known inn in the Middle Atlantic states. Set in the Tidewater area's richest bird hunting region, it is common in the fall to see a beautiful group of hunting dogs asleep on the Oriental carpet in front of the lobby fireplace. For all its size and elegance, the Tidewater is a country inn with an easy grace, comfortable rooms and a legendary dining room. Its menu is rich in local specialties such as poached eggs served over fresh crabmeat at breakfast, and Shrimp and Crabmeat Norfolk made with Smithfield ham. No one should even consider leaving the inn without having dined on their incomparable crab cakes, a Maryland specialty they have elevated to a fine art.

Nearby St. Michael's is an attractive port.

Courtesy Jared Coffin House/© Jim Elholm

BICKLEIGH COTTAGE, in Bickleigh, Devonshire, England, (near Tiverton), fulfills every traveler's dream of sleeping in a thatched cottage. This rambling inn sits in a classic English cottage garden along the banks of a glassy river. Through its small-paned windows guests can see a stone bridge and watch rabbits play on the riverbank.

Although Bickleigh Cottage serves only breakfast (the traditional English one of fresh farm eggs and bacon, home-baked breads and fine English preserves), there are two restaurants within sight. The local pub, with hearty pub meals and a convivial atmosphere, is across the street, and a fine restaurant sits right by the bridge.

The rooms are decorated in an eclectic English country style, with charming cottage furniture and Victorian pieces. What they lack in size and polish is made up for by a genuine country atmosphere. Admirers of old glass and china will especially like the collections showcased in the cabinets of the breakfast room.

THE JARED COFFIN HOUSE on Nantucket Island, Massachusetts, is the restored home of a wealthy ship owner. The lobby is an antique-filled parlor and each room is furnished with fine period pieces. Four other historic homes adjoining the Coffin House have been opened to increase the total number of rooms to fifty-eight. The newest of these, a Johnny-come-lately built in 1821, offers stunningly decorated rooms and a little more privacy than the main house.

The location of the Jared Coffin House is perfect for strolling the charming streets of the town and enjoying its gardens. In the spring the gardens are alive with tulips, daffodils, squills and phlox set against the bright spring greens of newly leafed trees and lawns. The gardens are accented by forsythia, magnolia and quince, which give way to forests of lilacs by mid-May. The windswept moors, dunes, beaches, antique shops, craft studios and classic views of shingled cottages and beach roses make the island a pleasure at any time of year.

Kitchen Metrics

For cooking and baking convenience, the Metric Commission of Canada suggests the following for adapting to metric measurement. The table gives approximate, rather than exact, conversions.

SPOONS	CUPS
1/4 teaspoon = 1 milliliter	1/4 cup = 50 milliliter
1/2 teaspoon = 2 milliliters	1/3 cup = 75 milliliters
1 teaspoon = 5 milliliters	1/2 cup = 125 milliliters
1 tablespoon = 15 milliliters	2/3 cup =150 milliliters
2 tablespoons = 25 milliliters	3/4 cup = 175 milliliters
3 tablespoons = 50 milliliters	1 cup = 250 milliliters

OVEN TEMPERATURES

200°F = 100°C	350°F = 180°C
225°F = 110°C	375°F = 190°C
250°F = 120°C	400°F = 200°C
275°F = 140°C	425°F = 220°C
300°F = 150°C	450°F = 230°C
325°F = 160°C	475°F = 240°C

TO ADAPT LENGTHS

one inch = 2.5 centimeters
one foot = 30 centimeters
one yard = .9 meters

TO ADAPT MASS

one ounce = 28 grams
one pound = .45 kilograms

Appendix

CHAPTER ONE

Appalachia
14440 Big Basin Way
Saratoga, CA 95070
Stenciled floor cloths

Braid Aid Fabrics
466 Washington St.
Pembroke, MA 02359
Rug braiding supplies

Country Curtains
The Red Lion Inn
Stockbridge, MA 01262
Curtains and linens

Dana Robes Wood Craftsmen
P.O. Box 707, Lower Shaker Village
Enfield, NH 03748
Shaker furniture

El Mercado Mexican Imports
P.O. Box 12196
San Antonio, TX 78212
Mexican rugs

Indian Pueblo Cultural Center, Inc.
2401 12th St., NW
Albuquerque, NM 87102
Navajo rugs

Kentucky Hills Industries
Pine Knot, KY 42635
Furniture

New England Stencil Co.
Box 253
Old Mystic, CT 06372
Stencils and supplies

The Plow and Hearth
560 Main St.
Madison, VA 22727
Fireplace utensils

Red Clover Rugs
Somerset Farm
RD 2, Box 4420
Bristol, VT 05443
Hooked rugs and supplies

The Tinsman at Herbitage Farm
686 Old Homestead Highway
Richmond, NH 03470
Custom pierced tinwork

Trujillo's Weaving Shop
Box 18-A
Chimayo, NM 87522
Woven rugs

Western Reserve
Antique Furniture Kits
Box 206A
Bath, OH 44210
Museum furniture kits

CHAPTER TWO

Adobe Gallery
413 Romero NW
Albuquerque, NM 87104
Indian baskets and art

Arctic Trading Co.
P.O. Box 910
Churchill, Manitoba
R0B 0E0 Canada
Eskimo and Indian art and handwork

The Carroll Journals
2515 E. 43rd St.
P.O. Box 23667
Chattanooga, TN 37422
English country decor

Folk Arts Center
Southern Highland
Handicraft Guild
Blue Ridge Parkway
Milepost 382
P.O. Box 9545
Asheville, NC 28815
Appalachian crafts

Frye's Measure Mill
RFD 1
Wilton, NH 03086
Firkins and Shaker boxes

Herbitage Farm
Old Homestead Highway
Richmond, NH 03470
Folk art kits

Homespun Weavers
530 State Ave.
Emmaus, PA 18049
Woven table linens

Iroqrafts
RR7H
Ohsweken Six Nations
Reserve, Ontario
N0A 1M0 Canada
Indian arts

The Margaret Cavigga
Quilt Collection
8648 Melrose Ave.
Los Angeles, CA 90069
Antique quilts and rugs

National Trust for
Historic Preservation
1600 H St., NW
Washington, DC 20006
Museum reproductions

Pickety Place
Nutting Hill Rd.
Mason, NH 03048
Herbal and country crafts

Quarry Road Studios
RFD 1, Box 10
Proctorsville, VT 05153
Handweaving and pottery

The Rosemary House
120 S. Market St.
Mechanicsburg, PA 17055
Potpourri supplies

Smith and Hawken
25 Corte Madera
Mill Valley, CA 94941
Raffia

Sweet Grass
445 Bishop St., NW
Atlanta, GA 30318
Furniture, folk art

CHAPTER THREE

Country Manor
P.O. Box 520
Sperryville, VA 22740
Pickling crocks

Jeff Miller, blacksmith
The Fort at No. Four
P.O. Box 336, Route 11
Charlestown, NH 03603
Iron corn drying trees, hand-forged hooks

Potpourri from Herbal Acres
Pine Row Publications
Box 428
Washington Crossing, PA 18977
Herb newsletter

Smith and Hawken
25 Corte Madera
Mill Valley, CA 94941
Herb drying racks

CHAPTER FOUR

Alberta Nurseries and Seed, Ltd.
P.O. Box 20
Bowden, Alberta
T0M 0K0 Canada
Herbs, vegetables

The Cook's Garden
P.O. Box 65
Londonderry, VT 05148
Seeds for salad greens

Gardener's Collection
Deline Lake, P.O. Box 243
Sydenham, Ontario
K0H 2T0 Canada
Stoneware garden markers

High Altitude Gardens
P.O. Box 4238
Ketchum, ID 83340
Short-season seeds

Johnny's Selected Seeds
Foss Hill Rd.
Albion, ME 04910
Vegetable seeds

Mrs. MacGregor's Garden Shop
4801 First St., N.
Arlington, VA 22203
Teak window boxes, garden accessories

Montana Exclusive
29 Border Lane
Bozeman, MT 59715
Rustic garden furniture

Plants of the Southwest
1812 Second St.
Santa Fe, NM 87501
Dry climate gardens

Richters
Box 26, Hwy. 47
Goodwood, Ontario
L0C 1A0 Canada
Herb/vegetable seeds, supplies

Shepherd's Garden Seeds
7389 W. Zayante Rd.
Felton, CA 95018
Varieties for container gardens

The Swinging Bridge Pottery
S.R. 2, Box 395
Criglersville, VA 22727
Stoneware garden markers, bird feeders

CHAPTER FIVE

Campmore
810 Route 17 N.
P.O. Box 999
Paramus, NJ 07653-0997
Reflector ovens, campfire cookware

The Colonial Keeping Room
P.O. Box 218
Fairfield, ME 04937
Wooden sled replicas

L.L. Bean, Inc.
Casco St.
Freeport, ME 04033
Pullsleds, cross-country ski equipment

CHAPTER SIX

Cherry Tree Toys, Inc.
P.O. Box 369
Belmont, OH 43718
Wooden shapes

Heartscents
P.O. Box 1674
Hilo, HI 96721-1674
Hawaiian natural wreaths

Joe's Vines and Wreaths
Route 3, Box 213
Butler, TN 37640
Vine wreaths, cones

Maine Balsam Fir Products
P.O. Box 123
West Paris, ME 04289
Small fir cones

Meadowsweet Herb Farm
Eastham Rd., Box 729
Shrewsbury, VT 05738
Dried flower decorations

Ruby Mountain Everlastings
Southwest Alder, Box 70
Alder, MT 59710
Dried plants and flowers

CHAPTER SEVEN

Abigail's
906 McClure St.
Victoria, British Columbia
V8V 3E7 Canada
Caren Craig
(604) 388-5363

Bickleigh Cottage
Bickleigh, Devonshire
England
08845-230

The Compass Rose
North Head, Grand Manan,
New Brunswick
E0G 2M0 Canada
Cecelia Bowden
(506) 622-8570

The Crystal River Inn
326 W. Hopkins
San Marcos, TX 78666
Mike and Cathy Dillon
(512) 396-3739

Grinkle Park
Easington, Saltburn-by-the-Sea
Cleveland TS13 4UB, England
Lisa Chapman
0287-40515

The Foothill House
3037 Foothill Blvd.
Calistoga, CA 94515
Michael and Susan Clow
(707) 942-6933

The Handfield Inn
St. Marc-sur-le-Richelieu, Quebec
J0L 2E0 Canada
(514) 584-2226

The Jared Coffin House
56 Centre St.
Nantucket, MA 02554
(508) 228-2400

Jasper Park Lodge
Jasper, Alberta
T0E 1E0 Canada
(403) 852-3301

Kent Manor Inn
Kent Island, MD 21666
Sarah Humphries
(301) 643-5757

The King's Cottage
1049 E. King St.
Lancaster, PA 17602
Jim and Karen Owens
(717) 937-1017

The O'Ban Inn
160 Front St., Box 94
Niagra-on-the-Lake, Ontario
L0S 1J0 Canada
Gary Burroughs
(416) 468-2165

The Old Rittenhouse Inn
Box 584, 301 Rittenhouse Ave.
Bayfield, WI 54814
Jerry and Mary Phillips
(715) 779-5765

The Orchards
222 Adam's Rd.
Williamstown, MA 01267
(413) 458-9611

The Patchwork Quilt Country Inn
11748 CR2
Middlebury, IN 46540
Michele Goebel
(219) 825-2417

Pleasant Street Inn
17 Pleasant St.
Rockport, MA 01966
The Norrises
(508) 546-3915

Rancho Caymus Inn
P.O. Box 78
Rutherford, CA 94573
Mary Tilden Morton
(707) 963-1777

The Tidewater Inn
Dover and Harrison Streets
Easton, MD 21601
(301) 822-1300

White Swan Tavern
231 High St.
Chestertown, MD 21620
(301) 778-2300

Index

Silhouetted Photographs

© Lynn Karlin; Artist Mr. Lord: p14
Courtesy Williams-Sonoma: p17 top
Courtesy Country Floors: p17 bottom
© Lynn Karlin; Sheepscot Stenciling: p22
© Lynn Karlin/Courtesy Country Living Magazine: p50
© Lynn Karlin/Courtesy Country Living Magazine: p53
© Lee Foster/FPG International: p79
© Steven Mark Needham/Envision: p81
Northwind Pictures Archives: p125
© Steven Mark Needham/Envision: p153